SOUTHERN MESSENGER POETS

Dave Smith, Series Editor

THE HOUSE ON
BOULEVARD ST.

New and Selected Poems

DAVID KIRBY

Louisiana State University Press
Baton Rouge

Published by Louisiana State University Press
Copyright © 2007 by David Kirby
Manufactured in the United States of America

Designer: Barbara Neely Bourgoyne
Typefaces: Whitman, text; Univers, display
Printer and binder: Edwards Brothers, Inc.

Library of Congress Cataloging-in-Publication Data
Kirby, David, 1944–
The house on Boulevard St. : new and selected poems / David Kirby.
p. cm. — (Southern messenger poets)
ISBN-13: 978-0-8071-3214-2 (cloth : alk. paper)
ISBN-13: 978-0-8071-3215-9 (pbk. : alk. paper)
I. Title. II. Title: House on Boulevard Street. III. Series.
PS3561.I66H69 2006
811'.54—dc22
2006013688

The paper in this book meets the guidelines for permanence
and durability of the Committee on Production Guidelines
for Book Longevity of the Council on Library Resources. ∞

Or ti riman, lettor, sovra 'l tuo banco,
   dietro pensando a ciò che si preliba,
   s'esser vuoi lieto assai prima che stanco.

So wait there, reader, on your bench,
   and think about what's coming,
   if you'd rather be happy than tired.

             —*Il Paradiso*, Canto X, 22–24

CONTENTS

III

PREFACE

As I plowed the soil whence these poems sprang, two old moles worked the earth beneath me. One was Shakespeare, whose compositional method helped me organize not only the whole book but also each separate section as a dream. The other was Dante: thanks to him, the book is divided into the three sections that give it a rough symmetry. Here, though, the sections deal with the heated restlessness of youth, the mixed blessings of self-imposed exile, and the settled pleasures of home, because, though I've spent the usual amount of time in purgatory, for the life of me I can't recall a single minute in hell and have passed many a day that comes close to being paradisal.

Most of these poems were written in the last fourteen years. The first of these longish narrative poems tell stories chronologically, whereas the later poems are likely to combine time periods in the manner of the mind rather than count them off as the clock does. All of the poems are marked by fixed-length stanzas and a sawtooth margin, effects intended to help with the sense of what one critic calls in these poems "the whole motion of the speaker's psyche: like a pendulum, it swings in one direction with an enthusiasm or passion, momentarily comes to a point of rest, and then swings back the other way."

A conventional *New and Selected* would begin with a selection of poems from past books and conclude with recent poems. Since this one is organized around the periods of time the poems explore rather than their dates of publication, I'll identify which old poems came from where and which poems are new.

These poems appeared in *My Twentieth Century* (Washington, DC: Orchises Press, 1999): "The Afterlife," "The Ghost of Henry James," and "Listening to John Crowe Ransom Read His Poetry."

These poems appeared in *The House of Blue Light* (Baton Rouge: Louisiana State University Press, 2000): "At the Grave of Harold Goldstein," "Dear Derrida," "The Exorcist of Notre-Dame," "For Men Only," "Heat Lightning," "The House of Blue Light," "Meetings with Remarkable Men," "My Dead Dad," "Roman Polanski's Cookies," "Strip Poker," and "Teacher of the Year."

These appeared in *The Ha-Ha* (Baton Rouge: Louisiana State University Press, 2003): "Americans in Italy," "Borges at the Northside Rotary," "Calling Robert Bly," "The Elephant of the Sea," "Everything You Do Is Wrong," "The Fugawi,"

"The Little Sisters of the Sacred Heart," "On My Mother's Blindness," and "The Search for Baby Combover."

The following poems are appearing in a book for the first time here, even though they appeared earlier in these magazines: "The Beauty Trap" (*Georgia Review*), "The House on Boulevard St." (*Mississippi Review*), "The Crab Nebula" (*Mid-American Review*), "Dead Girl Takes Packet Boat to Provincetown" (*Five Points*), "The Desperate Hours" (*Kenyon Review*), "A Fine Frenzy" (*Ploughshares*), "The Hand of Fatima" (*River Styx*), "I Think Satan Done It" (*Shenandoah*), "I Think Stan Done It" (*Denver Quarterly*), "My Brother the Jew" (*Southern Review*), "Occupation: Hero" (*Ninth Letter*), "The Laughter of Pigs" (*Paris Review*), "Seventeen Ways from Tuesday" (*Subtropics*), "Sex and Candy" (*Meridian*), "Stairway to Heaven" (*One-Trick Pony*), "Van Diemen's Land" (*Smartish Pace*), and "The Winter Dance Party" (*Southern Review*).

The quotations from *The Divine Comedy* that begin the book as well as each section of it were translated by me, sometimes with a liberality I should probably be ashamed of.

THE HOUSE ON
BOULEVARD ST.

Stairway to Heaven

After the show, Chris the lute player says
some people think there has to be a tight fit
            between text and music, which isn't true:
if both are good, then they go together
      whether they go together or not,
and as he's talking, I'm thinking, Makes sense,

      because I'd just read that the five components
of any magic act are appearance, disappearance,
            transformation, levitation, and sawing,
and while each of the first four of these has
      at least some relation to the other three,
they're all different from sawing,

      yet every magic act—every *good* magic act,
I should say—is full of surprises,
            is a "stairway of surprise," as Emily Dickinson
said about good poetry, if not precisely
      a "Stairway to Heaven," in the words
of the celebrated if rather terrible Led Zeppelin song.

      "Surprise, surprise!" says Gomer Pyle,
and Dante Alighieri, too, is both the surprisee
            of his own poem, caught out as he is
in the middle of the dark wood of the middle of his life,
      and its surprisor, conveying the reader
through Hell and Purgatory and up the Mount of Paradise

      the way every musician, magician, poet,
and songwriter hopes not only to surprise the listener,
            viewer, reader, and (again) listener but also
to lift that listener, etc., to the veriest Elysium,
      Valhalla, Nirvana, and Zion, as do I
when I begin to write poems in the manner of this one—

      these "memory poems," as I call them—even though,
at the time that I begin to write them,
            I'm not at all sure exactly what it is

1

that I am doing or even why. But then
        Roy Lichtenstein dies—Roy-who-went-from-
sober-Abstract-Expressionist-designs-

        to-kitschy-comic-book-characters-Lichtenstein—
and he is quoted in his obit as saying,
                "It's true that when I looked at what I was doing,
it offended my own sense of taste. . . .
        This was, without question, contrary to everything
one had been taught about matters of style and

        substance, and so forth. But once I did those
paintings, I couldn't work in any other way. . . .
                I didn't think anyone would be interested in them—
and I didn't really care. That part wasn't important.
        What was important was that I was doing them."
So this is helpful, having Roy's example.

        Part of the problem, of course, is that
I think I am inventing something totally new,
                for example, with the saw-toothed left margin
I start to favor, but then one day I am preparing for class
        and begin reading Marianne Moore and say,
Ohhhh, boy, because I see Marianne had beat me to it

        in the saw-toothed margin department. Even the term
memory poem isn't mine, since Byron had used it
                for some autobiographical poems of his own.
But then I begin to see little things
        I find helpful, such as this comment
on *Don Juan* by Virginia Woolf that I come across

        in the Byron biography I have been reading:
"It's what one has looked for in vain—
                an elastic shape which will hold whatever
you choose to put in it," and I think, Yes indeedy,
        these babies are nothing if not elastic!
And then I read something Donald Barthelme

had written, a 1974 note on his story "Paraguay":
"Mixing bits of this and that from various areas of
               life to make something that did not exist before
is an oddly hopeful endeavor," and certainly
      the phrase "oddly hopeful" describes not only
my memory poems but, well, my whole life, I guess,

      of which I am sort of making a braid,
though not exactly. And have you ever come across
               something you've written earlier that explains
what you're doing at the moment, even though
      there's no other connection between the two?
I do when I am looking through a file of old stuff

      and come across this review I'd written
of a collection of Hayden Carruth's essays
               called *Reluctantly* in which I'd said,
"these essays . . . start abruptly and ramble
      purposefully over the landscape before concluding
in a way that is both surprising and appropriate,"

      and I realize, hey, that's what the memory poems
are like! Or what they're like when they're good.
               Now a word about the titles: about the time
I begin to write these poems, I discover
      all these electronic databases I can access
from the computer they had given me at school,

      and I figure that although all of them asked
the user to research a topic using either the "Author,"
               "Keyword," "Subject," or "Title" function,
probably most users would use "Keyword"
      or "Subject," because if you know the title
of an essay and who wrote it before you start,

      why would you want to look it up in the first place?
So as I finish the memory poems, I give them
               what I call primal titles; for example, I call

my poem about polio "Polio" instead of, I don't know,
        "Nurses and Orderlies." Or if I write a poem
about John Crowe Ransom or Jacques Derrida,

        I use their names as titles instead of
calling the poems "Ah Fugitive!" or "Indeterminacy."
                So I am pretty confident about the whole project
even though nobody else has said much about it, and then
        this anthology appears with some memory poems in it,
and in her introduction, editor Judith Kitchen

        refers to "David Kirby's hilarious roundabout forays
into his own mind," and I figure, That's about right,
                because, like the chorus in a Greek play,
for the most part I watch the action and comment
        on it without being drawn into it—what I do
is *think* about it instead—though occasionally

        I put on my toga and step out into the footlights
and do a turn or two. I've always liked this quote
                from Ted Solotaroff which says that writing
is often a writer's "only way to organize
        and to some extent comprehend
life's fullness and perplexity," and I think

        a nice corollary to that is a remark
by Isaac Newton, who said he thought of himself,
                not as a great man, but as a boy playing
on the seashore and looking for a smoother pebble
        or a prettier shell than before.
Not that I'm like Isaac—more like Wayne Newton, say.

        Or a Fig Newton. Though each of these—
Isaac, Wayne, Fig—is true to itself, much in the manner
                of the thirteenth-century mason who is polishing
the foundation stones for Notre-Dame de Paris, and someone says,
        "Don't polish those things, no one will ever see them,"
and he shrugs and says, "Our Lady will."

I

"Guardaci ben! Ben son, ben son Beatrice.
   Come degnasti d'accedere al monte?
   non sapei tu che qui è l'uom felice?"

"Look hard: of course I'm Beatrice, of course I am!
   Why did you climb the mountain?
   Did you guess that people are happy here?"

—*Il Purgatorio,* Canto XXX, 73–75

"Fair Creatures of an Hour"

At my fortieth high-school reunion, the men have these big stomachs,
                    and the women have . . . brooches.
Butterflies, flowers, starfish, big gold salamanders: why? I want to say,
                    "What's with the brooches, girls!"
but then I'd just come across as Mr. Smarty Pants Poet,
                    Mr. Irony Boy, Mr. Ph.D. Even If He Doesn't Make
as Much as Y'all and Is Therefore, Like, Totally Envious and Hateful.

Many of our classmates aren't here: as A. E. Housman says,
                    a lot of athletes *do* die young, from cancer
or Vietnam. But the saddest are the ones who took their own lives:
                    Linda McCrain, who thought she was ugly
and put a shotgun barrel in the middle of her face, and Freddy Cangelosi,
                    dumped yet again by yet another girl
who dated him for his money and found by his parents in the family garage,

his Corvette still idling. They could have been happy. Didn't they know?
                    Couldn't they have waited? Frederika Moats
was the class "hot girl" because she had this great honker of a nose
                    and let boys treat her like trash,
but then she had plastic surgery the summer after graduation
                    and became chaste and modest
and found a guy in college who adored her, who adores her to this day.

Two of these women tell Barbara they really liked me because
                    I was "funny" and "nice," which kind of
depresses me, because it makes me think of all the girls I could have had
                    if I'd been "serious" and "nasty."
Remorse is the fatal egg by Pleasure laid, according to Cowper,
                    but, hey, no egg here—no remorse!
Okay, maybe there was a big open-mouthed kiss, one for each girl,

but shouldn't I have taken them out past the dairy farm to the pond
                    with the live oaks around it
on a hot July night and pressed my mouth to their bodies singly

or, omigod! together, the three of us sweaty
and laughing as the night's starry face beamed on our pale thighs?
                    Well, yeah, but then today they wouldn't
be telling Barbara what a fucking prodigy I am, would they?!?

Oscar Wilde says they fly through the dim purple air of Dante
                    who have stained the world
with the beauty of their sin. Oh, ha! I think I stained my world
                    with sunlight, maybe, or Liquid Paper!
I don't know, oxygen molecules—not sin, that's for sure.
                    Or not enough sin.
Surely death will come to us all and to those we love:

as the great Albert Goldbarth says, if the author of *The Divine Comedy*
                    died and Shakespeare, too,
who are we to say no? But will it be pretty? Will we say,
                    as Charlotte Brontë did,
that our loved ones are "gone like dreams," that one by one
                    we watched them fall asleep on our arm?
Will we be like Antonio Delfini, whose father went climbing

in the mountains, and it was a beautiful day, cold but sunny,
                    and then the weather changed,
and the father died in an avalanche, and decades later, his climber-son
                    went looking for him,
and he searched all over, and just as he was about to give up,
                    he looked over the lip of the little ledge
he stood on and there, in the grays and pinks of the day's last light,

he looked down and saw his father, years younger than he was,
                    asleep under the ice.
Maybe that's what all the brooches are for! To ward off death
                    or, since death can't be warded off,
to ward off painful death, protracted death, *ugly* death.
                    Maybe that's why all these women
are so happy: their salamanders are protecting them!

From the porch of Clayton Thomas's log-cabin palazzo,
             the Class of '62 waves good-bye.
Ten years from now, some of them won't be standing here.
             Someone is crying, though I can't tell who.
Then a car turns in the driveway; its headlights sweep the porch,
             and suddenly the dark is alive
with gold, silver, amethyst, diamonds as hard as stars.

At the Grave of Harold Goldstein

I'm at a graveside service for someone I didn't know,
     a Mrs. Goldiner, the mother of my friend Maxine,
who is sitting with her sisters Jill and Andrea
          and sniffling a little as the rabbi, who calls himself
"Rabbi" when he phones the house, as in
          "This is Rabbi" ("Don't you think that's primal?"
Maxine will say later. "Don't you expect someone
               in a robe and a staff in his hand?"),

          is saying how the dead woman grew up in Pennsylvania
     and went to New York and worked for Saks Fifth Avenue
and met her future husband at a party, and by now
          I'm daydreaming in sepia about the Lower East Side
and anxious first-generation immigrant parents
          and yeshiva boys and pigtailed girls in gingham dresses
               and storefronts and pushcarts and Model A Fords,

          when suddenly I realize that I'm standing by the grave
     of someone I did know, Harold Goldstein, who was
the dean of the library school at the university
          where I work and whom I liked a lot, a person
"of pure character," as his headstone says, and,
          continuing with the engraver's characteristic disregard
of punctuation, "lofty aims / life rich in generous
               regard for others, and devotion to publicity,"

          and I think, Well, that's one thing we had
     in common, and then I look again, and of course
it says, "devotion to public duty," not publicity,
          and for a moment I blush to think not only
of my exaggerated self-love but also of my eagerness
          to associate myself with someone as fine as
               Harold Goldstein, who, as far as I could tell,

          was pure, lofty, generous, and so on,
     whereas I, even in my late forties, am different
only in degree rather than kind from

the self-appointed j.d. of *anno Domini* 1961,
tough-guy-in-his-own-mind-only
who had but dreamed of genuine juvenile delinquency,
dreamed of being bad enough
to be sent by his parents to all-boys Catholic High,

which was part religious school and part
minimum-security detention center, since it contained
not only the sons of the faithful but also
most of the fuck-ups from the public schools,
who were now concentrated under one roof
and therefore in a position to learn additional vices
as well as pass on the ones they had already mastered

to such a one as I, who would digest far more
of the world's nastiness were he to be yanked summarily
from the cookies-and-milk milieu of Baton Rouge High
and set down without preamble among the brawlers,
purse snatchers, serial masturbators, and teen alcoholics
of dear old CHS, one of whom was the inestimable
Riley Tucker of this narrator's youth, which Riley,
having revealed his penchant for crime even earlier,

had been sentenced to terms in Catholic
elementary as well as junior high schools
and by now was specializing in the theft,
joyriding in, and abandonment of General Motors
vehicles—the bigger, the better, since his ordinary mode
of transport was not only shamefully legal
but small, a Renault with the engine in the back

and a two-tone town-and-country horn
that his father had given up for the Buick
that better matched his position in life,
whereas the Renault only mocked Riley's outlaw status;
worse, one of the conditions of his sentence
was that he had to take his sister to
her all-girl school, St. Joseph's, which she had
to attend as a parallel to Riley's incarceration,

though eventually he persuaded his mom to alternate days
with him so we could join the track team, our workouts
consisting less of stretching and running laps and more
of eating Hershey bars and drinking Seven-Ups and smoking
Riley's supply of shoplifted Chesterfields and Kools.
This one day I needed a ride home,
so after school I set out with Riley in the Renault,

and when we got to St. Joseph's, the girls were waiting
out front, most of them having undone the top buttons
of their blouses and pulled their plaid skirts up
and lain out on the lawn to enjoy the last of the sun
while they waited for their rides and listened to
the ineffectual cluckings of the elderly nun
whose job it was to see them off the premises,
and what happened next was that Riley

decided to "cut some maneuvers" in the Renault
so the girls could see how fabulous we were,
only, in the course of the zigs and the zags
and the zips, Riley spun the wheel so hard
that we found ourselves on the wrong side
of the little French car's notoriously high center
of gravity, and we ended upside down in the parking lot,

the Renault teetering nicely on its roof as Riley
and I huddled on our heads and shoulders and watched
Riley's sister get in their mother's car—where did *she* come from?—
and vanish. Standing at the grave of Harold Goldstein,
I can still see Riley's upside-down mother
giving us a single disgusted glance and then
driving away slowly, her car gliding as though fixed
to some futuristic monorail.

Suddenly there is a commotion: Rabbi has alluded
to the fact that Maxine's sister Andrea is pregnant
by her husband Charles, only Andrea too has been daydreaming
and thinks Rabbi has said "her husband Al,"

who is actually Maxine and Jill and Andrea's late father,
        so Andrea says, "Charles! Charles!" and the others say,
                "Rabbi said, 'Charles,' Andrea," and Andrea calms down.

            What was Riley's mother doing at St. Joseph's anyway?
        Obviously either she or he had got the day wrong,
but I'll never know, because the totaled Renault
            was towed and forgotten, and I,
guilty by association, walked everywhere for a year,
        though usually only down to the corner,
where I waited for Riley to come by in his latest acquisition,
            the theft of which I was also an accessory to,

            I suppose, even if we were never caught. My crimes
        are little ones these days, but I guess we should all
do the best we can, so it's probably good to have
            this kind of accident, by which I mean the unplanned
rediscovery of a person like Harold Goldstein,
        of which the world needs more, not less,
            and whose example I have resolved to emulate

            as much as my below-average character and mediocre aims
        permit, even though his way, the right-side-up way,
is not especially aesthetic, but why even think about
            aesthetics when things are falling apart all around you
and death and misunderstanding are on every side?
        Then again, in *Stardust Memories,* when Woody Allen
asks these wise space aliens who visit Earth
            if he shouldn't be performing more good deeds,

            they tell him that if he really wants to serve humanity,
        he should tell funnier jokes—wait, that's *my* duty,
I think, that's my public duty! Because sooner or later,
            we all turn upside down: you're zipping along nicely,
a hotshot, and everybody's checking you out, when boom,
        over you go. And look! There goes your mother!
            She's driving away slowly across the ceiling of the world.

Twist and Shout

Or *Twitch and Shout,* according to Lowell Handler's book
(New York: Plume, 1999) about Tourette Syndrome.
      Anyway, or, as the students say, anyways, when I call for
a taxi and the hold music turns out to be Junior Walker and
          the All Stars singing, "Shotgun, shoot 'em 'fore they run, y'all,

      do the jerk, baby, do the jerk now," I wonder:
just what exactly is the connection between killing and dancing?
      Why such a thin line between the agony and the ecstasy,
as they say over here in Italy, which is about when,
          because it's dinnertime and everybody wants a cab,

      the hold music changes to Elton John's "No Sacrifice,"
which makes it easy to shuffle back and forth in a sort
      of white-boy *merengue* and tap my one- and two-euro
pieces on the counter as I think how bitchy Sir Elton
          has been in the news lately, calling Taiwanese reporters

      "rude, vile pigs" and saying Madonna "should be shot."
So which is the real Sir Elton, king of the snake-hipped
      dance grooves or grumpy old frump? Also, when he
called the Taiwanese reporters "rude, vile pigs,"
          he then screamed, "Do you understand? Well, do you?"

      My analysis: yes, the reporters realized instanter
that Sir Elton abominated, loathed, detested, scorned,
      and despised them, if less from his forthright Anglo-
Saxon monosyllables than his wet-hen body language,
          his goggle-eyed, red-faced, cord-veined, shower-of-

      spittle, verge-of-a-subdural-hematoma, winkle-picker-
stomping, dog-kicking, personal-assistant-slapping
      fury. Did I say he was mad? "Every human life
is tossed backwards and forwards between pain
          and boredom," said the great Arthur Schopenhauer.

Yeah, like Sir Elton's, I'm so not thinking!
I'm about a hundred percent sure he passes his days
　　　　being brushed with peacock feathers and getting
foot rubs from twelve-year-old boys as personal
　　　　assistants with big red handprints on their cheeks

　　　　feed him demitasse spoonfuls of warm banana
pudding. No, no, I think the opinion of a second
　　　　great kraut-and-sausage-gnoshing thinker is more
applicable here, this being that of the equally great
　　　　Immanuel Kant, who pointed out that "humanity

　　　　is a crooked timber from which nothing straight
has ever been cut." Ha, ha! Very true, Immanuel!
　　　　For if our wood were pool-cue straight, if the bubble
of the carpenter's level lined up dead center every time
　　　　it's put on top of our heads by the parents, kids, teachers,

　　　　scoutmasters, lovers, and domestic animals who rely on
us to be obedient, loving, and gifted at math and knot tying
　　　　as well as generous with caresses and canned dog food,
then there'd be no such thing as the "abominable fancy,"
　　　　a phrase attributed by D. P. Walker in *The Decline of Hell*

　　　　(Chicago: U of Chicago Press, 1964) to nineteenth-century
preacher F. W. Farrar who was describing the centuries-old
　　　　Christian idea that the rapture of the heavenly few
is enhanced by their ability to see and enjoy the eternal torments
　　　　of the damned many, as though heaven and hell

　　　　were connected by closed-circuit television,
making the doughnuts the saints are dipping
　　　　in their glasses of skim milk all the sweeter
as the poxy sinners sizzle like 200-pound sausages
　　　　and pop and curl like six-foot-long bacon strips

　　　　while they roar, Tried to take control of the love,
the love took control of me! and Ah-whoo gawd!

and True fine mama, sho' like to ball!
Why, supreme rationalist Thomas Aquinas himself
        writes in the *Summa Theologica* (Venice: Nicolaus

        Jenson, 1480) that "in order that the happiness
of the saints may be more delightful to them and that they
        may render more copious thanks to God for it,
they are allowed to see perfectly the sufferings of the damned"!
        Kersplat! With that, a big crapload of misery

        is dropped on the already miserable by Tom the Bomb!
Even my new hero Benvenuto Cellini, who, upon being
        told by a haughty customer that he was a donkey, retorted
not only that he was a better man than that worthy
        in every respect but also that, if the fellow continued

        to provoke him, he, Benvenuto, would give him
harder kicks than any donkey would and who,
        on another occasion, told himself it would be all right
(it wasn't) to draw near the house of an enemy because
        "as it was Good Friday, I imagined that the madnesses

        of madmen might be giving themselves a holiday,"
even the great Benvenuto was not unsullied by
        the tar brush of religious bigotry, saying, upon finding
himself in jail with a man who "had been arrested
        as a Lutheran," that his cellmate was "an excellent

        companion," although, from the point of view
of his religion, "I found him the biggest scoundrel
        in the world." Hold on, though, reader—wait.
Just a second. Yes! I can see clearly now,
        the rain is gone. I see England, I see France,

        I see Benvenuto plain, running through life like
the rest of us, coursing over hill and dale
        like the Befana, the old gnarly Sicilian crone
at whose house the three wise men stop
        and who blows them off when they ask

if she wants to see the Christ child but then changes
her mind and runs after them with a sack of goodies,
        dropping some at every house with a child in it
to make sure she doesn't miss anybody.
        Everything that could have happened

        to Benvenuto did, yet even when his enemy
poisoned him, far from being vengeful, he thanked
        God that the noisome potion had been
given to him, for it cleansed Benvenuto of a "mortal viscosity"
        and thus "the poison worked so well that,

        whereas, before I took it, I had perhaps but three
or four years to live, I verily believe now that it has helped me
        to more than twenty years by bettering my constitution."
There's so little English for me to read in Italy
        that I even look at the oil futures in the *Tribune,*

        and this morning it says the price of "light, sweet crude"
has gone up, and I think, Light, sweet crude:
        now there's a nimble turn of phrase, if ever there was one,
and then I think of how it was when I went down to New Orleans
        for my draft physical with my friend Brody Saxon,

        who'd also been called, and how horrible that day was,
and how they stripped us down to our underwear,
        and a sergeant said, "Gentlemen, put your hands on your hip,"
which is when Brody yelled, "And let your backbone slip,"
        echoing "Land of a Thousand Dances" by Wilson Pickett

        as we examinees break up—we are pretty nervous already,
and probably anything would have done it, but we guffaw
        and pound each other and fall out of formation,
which drives the sergeants crazy, so that they run around
        screaming at us and treat us pretty roughly the whole rest

        of the day, as though we're in the army already,
yet every time a khaki-clad NCO shoves me through a door

or tells me to stand "like a man" or screams
"That's too many!" when I write "19" in the slot
      for "years in school" (excuse me, your honesty,

      but 12 years of the basics plus 4 of college and 3
of grad school equal 19, according to this raw recruit's
      thumb-and-finger method of addition), I think of Brody's
merry cry and say, Can I get a witness? to myself
      and then, Good God, y'all! and then, Somebody help me!

The Afterlife

       Shots and drafts? Ken would ask, and I'd say,
Shots and drafts, and off we'd go
       to some bar on Greenmount Street for jiggers
of cheap whiskey and ten-ounce brews,
       fresh from the tap, or just the beer itself:
most days we had to get up early
       and prepare for class or at least shuffle
our note cards so that when our advisers asked,
       How's the dissertation coming?
we could say, Fine, I was just working on it,

       and while a few beers never interfered with
our scholarly activities, such as they were,
       there is something about cheap whiskey
that makes you want to throw furniture
       through the window after a while—
which we never did, although fighting
       that impulse can be just as exhausting—
so we'd usually save the shots for an occasion,
       like the anniversary of the first edition
of *Leaves of Grass* or Fats Domino's birthday,

       and even our beer drinking came to be
rather systematic after a while:
       Johns Hopkins U. was a real pressure cooker,
and one way to deal with all the craziness
       was to make a few rules for yourself
and stick to them and then, when your own rules
       were making you as crazy as the ones
the professors were imposing, to go off the tracks
       for a while but then get back on
as soon as possible and with little damage done,

       which is why we (a) always walked to the bar,
(b) never made eye contact with anybody
       who was looking for an argument,
and (c) drank as much as we wanted

as long as we got home by one.
Whereupon we would make cinnamon toast:
        you're always hungry after you've been
drinking on an empty stomach,
        so I'd say, How about I heat up
some soup, or, A sandwich would be good about now,

        but Ken was insistent and usually got his way.
He had a sweet tooth, and also I figured
        maybe it was something everybody did in Detroit,
where he was from and about which I didn't know
        anything, being from Baton Rouge and thinking
that anyone who came from a bigger city
        was bound to know more about life than I did.
Besides, Ken did all the work:
        he'd turn on the oven and get out the butter
and the cinnamon and the sugar

        and prepare the bread slices and yank
the broiler rack out and put the slices
        on the rack and shove it back in,
and while we were waiting,
        we would talk about one of the Henrys,
Adams or James, or our professors
        or girls and how we wish we knew some,
and we would brew tea, which was
        Ken's other big passion after cinnamon toast,
or have another beer if there was any.

        And then we'd smell smoke,
because we always burned the first batch
        of toast, though far be it for fellows
as chuckleheaded and unflappable as we were
        by that point to become discouraged:
Ken would shout, Get the window, Kirbs!
        and I would raise the sash,
and he would grab a fork
        and yank out the broiler rack again,
and there would be all this cremated bread—

a dozen slices, maybe, because Ken loved
his toast, so we would make as much
        as would fit on the rack, and I'd eat
a couple of slices, and he'd have the rest,
        but only after he'd pitched the first batch
out the window: he'd get down
        in a three-point stance and, with coordination
uncommon to someone who had been drinking
        all night, start forking those charred slices
out the window, counting as he went:

        One! Two! Three! And when the last one
was gone, he'd put the fork down,
        dust his hands off exaggeratedly,
grin as if to say, That's that,
        and start on batch number two,
which always came out fine, because by that time
        we were alert to the hazard of overdoing it,
which we nonetheless did anyway, say,
        twice a week for the year that we roomed together
for a total of maybe a hundred times.

        Now this was not that big a deal in our lives
and certainly pales in comparison to
        a lot of things I remember from grad school,
but what I've always wondered is this:
        our apartment was on the top floor
of an eight-story building right by campus,
        and people were always hustling past at every hour
of the day or night, so if Ken
        forked a dozen slices of burned cinnamon toast
out the window every third day or so,

        there must have been people passing by
and being hit and saying to their friend,
        You get hit by something?
And the friend bends down and picks
        up this flat square and turns it over
and smells it and says,

Yeah, it's a piece of cinnamon toast.
And since most people are creatures of habit
        and take the same streets at the same time,
you have to imagine a couple of people

        going by in March and talking about Nietzsche
or the categorical imperative,
        and suddenly all this toast comes flying down,
and they look at the sky in disbelief
        and then brush each other off and keep going,
but a month later they're coming by again,
        lost in a discussion of structuralism
or the bicameral brain,
        when suddenly another shower of toast falls,
and they look at each other and say, Damn!

        Or I can picture somebody saying to his friend,
Come on, we're having a great time, let's go back
        to my place and make coffee, and the friend says,
Yeah, but don't go down Charles Street. . . .
        Or say someone is having a crisis because,
as Erik Erikson says, he half-realizes
        he is fatally overcommitted to what he is not.
Or, like Madame de Sévigné, a woman says
        that what she sees tires her
and what she does not see worries her,

        and they're walking along,
things have been up and down
        in their lives lately, but they're down now,
that's for sure, and they're thinking,
        God, why bother, and then the first piece
of toast hits them on the shoulder,
        and another piece lands in the bushes
a few feet away, and they look up,
        and pow, a piece hits them right on the nose,
but it's only cinnamon toast,

so it doesn't really hurt, and they pick it up,
and this piece isn't burned so badly,
        it's one of the ones that was in the front corner
of the broiler rack, and it's still warm,
        and the person is a little hungry because
he or she hasn't been eating so well lately,
        so they figure, What the hell,
and they take a little nibble,
        and it's not so bad, and they walk home
munching the warm cinnamon toast,

        and when they get there,
their husband or wife or lover says,
        Jesus, where have you been,
I was so worried, especially with
        the state of mind you've been in lately,
and the person gives a little smile—
        not a big one, because it's not as though
anything has really changed yet—
        and says, Well, you know,
the funniest thing just happened to me,

        and they sit down and have a long talk
and then get into bed together and keep talking
        and they don't really make love but they do kind of
nibble on each other and exchange big wet
        open-mouthed kisses and finally fall asleep
in each other's arms saying, Good night, I love you,
        good night, I love you so much, good night,
good night, and while this isn't the kind of scenario
        that you see in a lot of literature—a few stories
by Raymond Carver, say, or I. B. Singer—

        nonetheless any number of contemporary paintings
depict something very much like this kind of moment:
        an astonished throng looking skyward, say,
as a gigantic flock of wingéd toast blocks out

the stars and the moon. And this is just the type
of thing you want to happen when nothing
        is fun anymore and you know you have
to make a change but you don't know how
        and you can't help thinking,
There's got to be more to life than this.

Dear Derrida

My new grad-school roommates and I are attending
our first real lecture, which has gone okay,
we guess, since none of us understands it,
when one of our professors rises,
a somewhat prissy fellow
with a mild speech impediment,
and says he takes issue with the speaker's tone,
which he characterizes as one of "sar, sar,"
and here he raises his voice a little,
"sar, sar, sar," and wipes his mouth

with a handkerchief, "sar," and turns red
and screams, "sar, sar, sar—DAMN EET!—sarcasm!"
The four of us look at each other
as if to say, hmmmm, nothing like this
at the cow colleges we went to!
After that, whenever we'd spill our coffee
or get a sock stuck in the vacuum cleaner,
we'd look at the mess ruefully
and say, "da, da, da—SARCASM!—damn eet!"

Our lives were pretty tightly sealed,
and if we weren't in class or the library,
we spent our time either in wordplay
or cooking: what with girlfriends
and passersby, we always had a pot
of water boiling on the back of the stove
(it's like you're ready to deliver babies,
somebody said once), for spaghetti, usually,
or sausages, though one evening Chris,
the English student from England, came by

for a sausage supper, and after he left,
we ran up on the roof to pelt him
with water balloons, though when we did,

he fell down as though he'd been shot,
and one of us said, Jeez, what's wrong
                    with Chris, and somebody else said,
You know, Chris eats nothing but sausage,
                    and a third party said, Hmm,
          maybe we ought to vary our diet a little.

                    And that was our life: school, the boiled messes
          we made on that stove, and hanging around
that crummy apartment talking about,
                    I don't know, Dr. Mueller's arm,
I guess, which hung uselessly
          by his side for reasons no one
fathomed—polio, maybe, or some
                    other childhood disease—though Paul
said he thought it was made of wood.
          Can't be made of wood, said Michael,

you can see his hand at the end
                    of it, to which Paul replied,
Yeah, but you can have a wooden arm
          and a real hand, can't you?
And that was what our life was like,
                    because mainly we just sat around
and speculated like crazy while
                    the snow piled up outside,
          so much so that by the time spring came,

                    I'd had it, so I moved out of there and in with Grant
          and Brian and Poor Tom, who were philosophy
students but also genuine bad asses,
                    believe it or not, because at that time
you more or less had to be an existentialist,
          i.e., tough, and not a deconstructionist,
which was a few years down the road yet
                    and which would have left everyone
paralyzed, since all texts
          eventually cancel themselves out.

Of the new roomies, I hit it off best
                    with Grant, who became one of the big-brother
types I seemed to be looking for at that period in my life,
            and in fact he rescued me
on more than one occasion, such as the time I was talking
                    to a local girl outside a bar
called Jazz City and her three brothers
                    decided to "teach me a lesson" and would have
            if Grant hadn't punched one of them

                    across the hood of a parked car, or the night
            he and I were in this other place where
a biker gang called Quantrill's Raiders
                    hung out and into which wandered
a well-dressed couple so unaware
            of their surroundings that they asked the bartender
to please make them some hot toddies,
                    which set everybody to laughing,
only the Quantrills decided we were laughing at them
            and jumped up to "teach us a lesson"

and would have, too, if Grant had not thrown
                    a table at them and dragged me
out of there to dive behind some garbage cans
            and choke on our own laughter
while the drunk, fucked-up bikers howled
                    and swore and punched each other since they
couldn't punch us. All this was therapy,
                    I figured, since grad school was stressful enough
            to send three people I knew to the clinic

                    with barbiturate overdoses (two made it,
            one didn't), and I'm not even listing here
all the divorces I know of that were directly
                    attributable to that constant pressure
to be the best, be publishable, hireable,
            lovable, that came from professors and sweethearts
and parents but mainly from ourselves,

as though each of us were two people,
a good and capable slave, on the one hand,
        and, on the other, a psychotic master

who either locked us up with our pots
                of boiling water or sent us out to dance
with the devil in the streets of Baltimore.
        That year magi appeared from the East:
Jacques Lacan, Tzvetan Todorov,
                Roland Barthes, and Jacques Derrida
brought their Saussurean strategies
                to the Hopkins conference on "The Language
of Criticism and the Sciences of Man,"

                where they told us that all language
        is code and thus separate from reality,
and therefore everything
                is a text as long as there is nothing
more than this half-conscious
                linguistic interplay between perceiver
and perceived, which is another way
                of saying that language is the only reality
or at least the only one that counts.
        As different as these thinkers are,

each was telling us that there is no us:
                that cultural structures
or the media or Western thought
        or the unconscious mind
or economic systems make us
                what we are or what we seem to be, since,
in fact, we are not, which isn't such bad news,
                if you think about it, because it means
we don't have to take ourselves so seriously.

                Derrida and company make it impossible
        for anyone today to read a book
as they had before, but we didn't know that then.

Grant didn't, that's for sure;
four years later, he put a gun in his mouth
        and blew the back of his skull off,
and sometimes it makes me sad
                when I think of how long it takes
for new ideas to catch on, because,
        yeah, deconstruction might have saved us.

The Fugawi

I'm walking up Park toward Grand Central
        when the second prostitute in as many blocks says,
"Hey, Dave! Wanna date?" and I, attending
                my first meeting of the Modern Language Association,
pause open-mouthed and say, "You—you know me?

Did—did you listen to my paper on foreshortening
        in Henry James's novels?"
but then I realize I've left my nametag on,
                and suddenly my lovely brass-buttoned navy blazer
morphs into a pair of faded bib overalls,

and a straw hat appears on my head
        as a front tooth goes mysteriously missing. . . .
It's me, folks, Hickus Americanus,
                just off the boat he poled up the East River from Dogpatch
and tethered to the dock at the end of Fulton Street,

crying, "Hootie-hoot!" as he makes his way
        over the whitebait, the sea bass, the cod, pollack, flounder,
and mackerel, the pike and wall-eye, "Hootie-hoot, y'all!
                It's me! It's Dave! Y'all know me?
The buildings sure is tall here! I love yooouu! Hootie-hoot!"

Back on Park, the people I am with
        are laughing at me—hard.
Some are actually *weeping* and wiping their eyes,
                while others hold their stomachs and go, "Bleh-heh-heh!"
and I want to say to them all,

Laugh while you can, my overeducated amigos—
        nobody even snickered when I said,
"Insurance investigator," as Mrs. Carruth went around
                our eighth-grade classroom asking everybody
what they wanted to be when they grew up,

because in those days there were these matchbooks
        advertising the correspondence course you'd take
to learn how to shadow people, lift prints, detect lies,
                and the ad promised good pay, steady work, prestige,
and there was even a picture of a guy who looked like our dads—

better than our dads, even, more like Fred MacMurray
        in *Double Indemnity* with the fedora and the snappy patter
and the dame who'd eventually betray him.
                My dad was an English professor, and I, not wanting
to be him, became him. The suit I'm wearing on Park

cost forty bucks when I was a senior in college,
        and people compliment me on being able to wear it
even now, decades later, but the truth is I was pretty chunky
                back then, I lived on cheeseburgers and Budweiser,
and it's only now, after years of job stress

and meal skipping, that I'm able to get back into
        that suit again—not thanks to sandwiches and beer
this time but to *foie gras* and expensive Bordeaux.
                Same suit, different guy—or not? Stanley Kubrick said,
"Gentiles don't know how to worry":

could be I am congenitally unable
        to figure these things out, am a member
of the tribe so stupid that it wandered
                the hills and valleys crying, Where the Fugawi?
And do we know, and do we want to know,

and if we do, are we not like the doting husband
        who realizes to his horror that the alabaster body
of his beloved is a "dormitory from hell"
                harboring six alternate personalities, all of whom
have distinct identities, voices, even appearances

and who is told by her therapist, Yeah, sure,
        I can make her core personality step out of that inferno,

but what you get in the end might not be
              the darling you married, might be the kleptomaniac,
the arsonist, the crazy nun, the nympho?

When the Roman mob chased Cinna the poet,
          crying, "Kill him, he's a traitor!"
he answered, "I'm not Cinna the politician,
              I'm Cinna the poet!" and the mob cried,
"Kill him for his bad verses!"

and as I think of that, I can feel my jeans and T-shirt loosen
          and pull away and become a toga, then a pair of overalls,
then a brown gabardine sports coat as I say, "I'm Cinna the poet,"
              then, "Hootie-hoot!" then, "Okay, lady,
just where were you when the officers found his corpse?"

The Crab Nebula

"Sons of bitches," I say under my breath, "I'll kill 'em!"
        as I grade my students' papers and think, Okay,
they don't know how to use the semicolon,
        but these days neither do writers for the *New York Times,*
           not to mention the *Tallahassee Democrat;*

        still, what's with "Anyways, I'm going to lay down"
           and "She gave it to Cody and I," not to mention
"Dakota's going to lay down next to Cody and I"?
        Sonofabitching bastards. And then I remember
           what Hilton Als said about how Richard Pryor

hated white people, how, for black people,
        white people are like babies you have to take care of,
and they throw up on you again and again,
        but you can't punish them, because they're babies,
           and that's what my students are, babies. Bastards.

When I first started teaching at Florida State,
        I saw a sign for a "happening" in the Union Ballroom,
so I go over, and the leader puts us through some movement
        and centering exercises and then tells us to close our eyes,
           mill around, then open and reach for the nearest person,

with whom we'll then spend the rest of the day.
        So I close my eyes and claw the air until I feel
a pair of hands and these big bosoms, only it's this woman
        who begins to scream when she sees I'm her partner:
           "I wanted it to be my boyfriend!" she yells,

and now I have to spend the rest of the day
        with this angry woman, who also towers over me.
Both she and I look around for the boyfriend,
        but he's lying low, probably happy to be
           at some distance from this ill-tempered giantess.

Now this is "frost in July," as Emerson said
            in his essay on Montaigne, this is a "blow from a bride"!
And I think Emerson meant a chaste Congregationalist bride,
        not one of those brawlers we read of today.
            I've always envied people who know they're right

and you're wrong: "If you see a Bulgarian on the street,
            beat him," goes the Russian saying; "he will know why."
Well, not this Bulgarian! Not always, at least.
        Well, sometimes. Actually, I do know why people
            don't like me or I them: it's just chemistry,

    just the whirling gases and red dwarves and supernovas
            of the Crab Nebula making new worlds but also
no worlds, diamonds and lumps of coal,
        happy people and crabby people.
            Proximity, preference, prestidigitation:

    Miles Davis said that listening to so-called third stream
            music, which is a fusion of classical European music
with such jazz elements as improvisation,
        was akin to "looking at a naked woman that
            you don't like." But I'm sure there were naked women

    Miles liked to look at quite a bit! Just as I'm sure
            that the critic who described the exhibition
featuring work by Renoir and other Impressionists
        as "a cruel spectacle of works by . . . lunatics"
            would have characterized paintings more

    to his taste as "a considerate spectacle of works
            by . . . a bunch of sane guys" or, you know,
words to that effect. Let's face it—
        the tall woman just didn't like me.
            Elle ne m'aimait pas, also *non ho piacuto*

    alla signorina, and so forth and so on in all the major
            and minor languages. My crime is that I am myself.

34

Voltaire longed for the day when the last king
        would be strangled with the entrails
                of the last priest, but when that happens,

        we'll have to be our own kings and priests,
                for someone must rule us, say what to do,
tell us which fork to eat with. Some of the chilliest pages
        I've ever read contain the account of
                the badly damaged whaleship *Peggy*

        and her weak and starving crew who decided
                to eat one of their numbers; Captain Harrison
records that he was helpless to prevent them
        and so had to listen to the terrifying sounds
                of the execution and subsequent feast

        in the cabin next door. A few days later,
                the men began to look for another man to kill,
even though the captain said their shipmate's death
        had done them no service, that they were
                as emaciated and greedy as ever,

        and so it is for us lawless, ungoverned,
                self-directed so-and-sos, at least for the short term.
The great Georg Christoph Lichtenberg said that
        a book is a mirror, and if an ape looks into it,
                an apostle is hardly likely to look out.

        And if that's true of a book, then it's doubly true
                of someone else's face! Ha, ha!
When the big angry girl's boyfriend appears
        at last, he is taller than she is and
                much happier to see her than I'd have thought.

        They're parents by now, maybe even grandparents.
                Or divorced and remarried, probably to other people
or maybe even to themselves again.
        Love is all you need, as the Beatles said
                at just about this same time in the fabulous history

of this curious race of ours. I'd say love, sure, but other qualities
as well: on Wednesday mornings, I tutor
a kid at a school whose corridors have names like "Attitude Avenue,"
though my favorite of them all is "Perseverance Street."
Oh, and you need luck, which, like justice, is blind.

The Ghost of Henry James

"Enchantée!" says Mrs. Huntington, extending her hand,
                 which I take, my jaw dropping onto my chest
and my brain going into gridlock
         as I tell myself, Think, Kirby, say something,
anything, but I'm just standing there like an idiot,

"there" being the courtyard of the Villa Mercede
                 on the hill of Bellosguardo outside Florence,
a palazzo known as the Villa Castellani when Henry James
         not only lived in it but set part of
The Portrait of a Lady there, its heavily stuccoed

and cross-barred windows still suggesting,
                 as it did when I first saw it two months earlier,
"the mask, not the face of the house,"
         a place easy to get into, thinks Isabel Archer
to herself, yet, once in, impossible to leave—

for me, impossible to enter, or so I thought that first time,
                 so it was back down the hill to the city
and my students and class prep and lots of lovely meals
         and long, cold (but lovely) walks,
and then one night a woman comes by

(I don't have a phone) and introduces herself
                 as Cherry Barney, who is a friend of a friend,
and promises to send her husband Steve to pick me up
         (I don't have a car, either) for dinner one night,
and when Steve comes, we make embarrassed small talk,

like, "Uh . . . where do you live?"
                 the answer to which is, "Oh . . .
up in Bellosguardo," to which I say, "Do you know
         the Villa Mercede?" and Steve answers, "Oh,
I live there!" So that's where I dine that night,

in this big gloomy high-ceilinged place with
                    paved tile floors and curious partitions here
and there that no doubt destroyed the shape of some
          marvelous rooms to make modern-day apartments,
but the best part is meeting this woman named

Mrs. Huntington, Steve and Cherry's landlady,
                    who is 85 yet as lively as can be, confiding,
in French-accented English (she'd been born
          in Boston yet raised on the Continent) that
she "remeembaired playing at zuh feet of Monsieur

Henri Jame when he pay zuh veezeet," and I'm
                    thinking, whoa, is this possible? It's 1973
at the moment, and a little quick subtraction
          suggests she was born in 1887,
so, yeah, maybe she had been around—

James began *The Portrait* in 1880 but returned
                    to Florence in 1887, 1890 (when she would have
been three), and 1899 (twelve), so, sure,
          she could 'ave play at zuh feet of Monsieur Henri
when he pay zuh veezeet. The problem is

that I am doing this moron-level arithmetic
                    when I should be asking Mrs. Huntington
about her impressions, to use one of James's
          favorite words, the little essences,
something he said, say. But hell, no:

I'm standing there holding her hand
                    like she's a statue and going five from three
is eight, carry the one. . . .
          And by the time I get the dates right,
she has already make zuh retreat into zuh shadow.

So the next day it's dut-dut-dut-dut
                    like a cartoon character to the library,

where I grab vol. I of HJ's letters and read
        "a large handsome apartment in town
in the same house as the Huntingtons"

(to HJ, Sr., on 26 Oct. 1869) and then
                "the Huntingtons, who were blooming
in their ruddy beauty" (to Elizabeth Boott,
        the real-life basis for Isabel Archer,
on 10 Dec. 1873), which familiar language

one uses only to describe friends
                of long standing, people one sees
again and again as one comes and goes
        and has lunch and tea and dinner
and plays badminton and croquet and watches

the children grow up and get married
                and have their own children who, decades later,
will remeembair play at zuh feet
        of cher Monsieur Henri
when he pay zuh goddamn veezeet!

So as soon as I can, I make a date to go back
                and take tea with Steve and Cherry,
and this time I have all the questions
        I was too dumbstruck to ask before,
like not what did he look like, which I knew already

from portraits, but how was his voice: high? Low?
                How low? Was he hesitant or determined?
Did he like kids? Did he like you?
        But when I get to the Villa Mercede,
Mrs. Huntington is gone. "Gone?" I ask Steve.

"Gone," he says. "Gone where?" I say.
                "Don't know," he says. It seems that Steve
was walking back up the hill from town
        one afternoon and saw the portière driving
Mrs. Huntington to the station; the car

had lots of bags on top, and when Steve
                    asked the portière where Mrs. Huntington
had gone, the portière waved his hand vaguely
              towards the north and said "*Aldilà*,"
which Steve thought was a town for a couple of days

until he figured out that what the portière
                    had said was "*al di là*," which means
"beyond" or "outside," and that what the portière
              was doing was being protective of Mrs. Huntington
and not blabbing her whereabouts to just anyone,

especially Steve, who was a foreigner.
                    So there went my chance to question
the one person I was ever likely to meet
           who knew Henry James personally,
although at least I got to shake her hand.

And maybe she wouldn't have told me anything
                    anyway. It's not as though she was knocked out
to make my acquaintance; she was nice on the surface
              but reserved, too, as James himself was said to be:
the kindest man in the world, really,

though if you started getting into his business,
                    he would pull back into his shell
faster than a turtle; plus he wrote all those stories
              like *The Aspern Papers* which warn scholars
against snooping into writers' lives.

Still, I am pretty downcast,
                    but Steve and Cherry give me several cups of tea
as well as a big slice of panettone,
           the Christmas cake with the currants in it,
and I am feeling a good deal better

as Steve and I take a stroll in the garden
                    behind the villa and I turn and look up

just in time to see a man come out on the balcony
   of one of the apartments and scowl at us—
not "scowl," exactly, but "gaze down sardonically"

or something like that, this tallish man, dignified,
    portly in a way that says presence, not dissolution,
and peeved, perhaps, but mainly bemused,
   pursing his lips and knitting his brows
the way James does in the famous Sargent portrait,

and while he is obviously one of the other tenants,
    I say, "Who's that guy?" and Steve says—
and I have to hand it to him,
   it couldn't have been better if I'd planned it myself—
Steve says, "What guy?"

Meetings with Remarkable Men

My own heroes are not Andrew Jackson or John Bunyan
                or Cervantes but people I already know,
like Officer John Moore, the little skinny yellow-eyed guy
                who used to be what was called a "prize fighter"
(if you asked him, he'd think about it for a while and then say
                his biggest match was for $10,000 in 1947 against
Wild Bill Kelly) and who now writes parking tickets
                for the football players who leave their Broncos
in the handicapped spaces outside the Williams Building
        everyday so they don't have to walk far
to the desks where they'll drowse through
                my Contemporary Poetry class,

        and believe me, these behemoths are not too particular
                about what they say to Officer John when they catch him
in the fulfillment of his duties, but since,
                chin in hand, I've been watching him from my window
for years as he writes those tickets, he must be
                good at it, i.e., must be pleasing to his master,
the chief, so one day I say to him, "Officer John,
                what's your secret?" and he says, "Never stop writing,"
and I say, "Hmmm?" and he says, "Never stop writing!"
        and, in fact, he is writing a ticket
even as he is saying this to me, thereby providing
                a practical demonstration of his adage.

        So was Melville a wife beater? I hope not,
                because I love him, too, or at least I love the Melville
who ended Chapter 26 of *Moby-Dick* with this prayer:
                "If, then, to meanest mariners, and renegades
and castaways, I shall hereafter ascribe

high qualities . . . then against all
mortal critics bear me out in it, thou just Spirit
of Equality, which hast spread one royal mantle
of humanity over all my kind! . . . Thou who,
in all Thy mighty, earthly marchings, ever cullest
Thy selectest champions from the kingly commons;
bear me out in it, O God!"—also a nice thought,

better than "Never stop writing!" probably,
because a writer can certainly keep writing
the same junk over and over again,
and here I think of another guy I like to think of,
and another boxer, too, as it turns out,
a fellow I used to see sometimes in Baton Rouge,
a Golden Gloves champ and one even smaller
than Officer John, like, in the 105-pound-and-under
class, and he used to sit at the bar in the Pastime
after workouts and nurse a beer, and he looked just awful,
as though he were crying, his hair a mess
and his face red from his sparring partner's gloves,

and he'd sit there and drink that beer, and sometimes
these bullies would pick on him, call him a faggot
and push him and push him, and then sometimes actually
physically *push* him, whereupon this little unassuming
red-faced mosquito of a human being would step down
carefully from that stool, and his arms would become
a blur in front of the bully's face and mid-section,
and you'd hear this faint sound, kind of like
a sewing machine in the next room, and after
thirty seconds or so of this, the bully would
go over backwards and hit the floor of the Pastime
and lie there like a pizza somebody had dropped,

and while I'm not in favor of beating
the other fellow about the mandibles
as a solution to every problem, still,
I like to think of that little mighty atom of a guy,

that pocket Hercules, and his gift to us all
                of that one element so largely absent
from our quotidian existence, i.e., surprise,
                and now I'm remembering the time I got the jolt
of my life and almost my death when I was seventeen
        and jogging at the track at LSU where my high-school team
worked out, the spotty teens mixing freely
                with the burlier college athletes,

        and suddenly I hear myself go PHHRRGGMUH!
                as my hips shoot forward and my head snaps back
toward my heels: I have just been tackled by
                1958 Heisman Trophy–winning fullback Billy Cannon,
a star sprinter in the off season and one now
                pointing at a javelin quivering in the earth
not ten feet away, the arc of which spear
                having been transected by the body
of your correspondent only seconds earlier,
        prompting the moralizing gladiator
to observe, "That ought to be a learner!"
                and it was, too, as in, Heads up, Dave!

        Which just goes to show you that the author
                of *Moby-Dick* is right, there's plenty to learn
from the cops and boxers and fullbacks of this world.
                Poor Mrs. Melville! It can't have been easy
to be married to a solitary hemorrhoidal genius.
                I don't know if Officer John or the little boxer
or Billy Cannon ever married at all,
                but if they did, I hope they were heroes
to their wives as they are to me,
        though I doubt it, since for most of us
a hero has to be somebody familiar but not too.
                Herman, Herman, please be sweet to your Elizabeth.

Van Diemen's Land

I'm walking behind my friends after a night on the town,
and they're not only *shambling* but weaving from side to side,
sometimes together, like over-the-hill soul singers
trying to regroup after years of pursuing failed solo careers,
and sometimes in different directions, like criminals

who've forgotten they're chained together,
like sailors on their last night of shore leave before a voyage to,
I don't know, Van Diemen's Land, and they'll lose their fingers
in the rigging, and their teeth will fall out,
and they'll be flogged so hard they won't remember their own names.

So much pain out there, and almost none of it ours.
The sailors had plenty of it, and so did the aborigines
sleeping naked as babies on the banks of the Ouse
until the white men arrived, hungry and scared
and toothless and looking for somebody to take it out on.

Once my father asked me if I knew what S&M was,
and I was too embarrassed to say yes, so I said no,
and he said he thought it might stand for "Sadism & Masochism,"
but if that's the case, why not just say so?
Why don't people say what they mean? Why don't they *behave*?

Even in our time, the world is a choir of angels one day,
and the next thing you know, it's the Raft of the Medusa,
with neither boat nor land on the horizon, not even a bird
in the air to throw a stick at, and everyone
is sizing everyone else up, wondering who's weak enough to eat.

They're still shambling, the guys, and not like first-time shamblers,
either. At least they're not vomiting. That's the worst, isn't it,
vomiting? One minute you're making the most divine conversation,
like Jeremy Northam in some Regency comedy of manners,
the next you're horking up the contents of your entire stomach.

Now the children of the sailors' sons and daughters are married
to the children of the daughters and sons of the Big River tribe,
        and Van Diemen's Land is Tasmania, that is to say, Australia.
Yesterday a student told me he likes to take the "drunk bus"
    because "it's fun and you can meet girls on it—drunk girls."

        We're not allowed to meet drunk girls, my friends and I,
and the drunk girls know it; they sail past in their expensive cars,
        and none stops. God, see us to our beds—that's your job!
And you, Sergeant Sleep, lay on us your scourge,
    your knout, your flail, your lash, your many-headed cat.

Strip Poker

       I'm giving blood and looking at a magazine photo
of bosomy Ava Gardner next to that squirt Sinatra
       and remembering saying, "Want to play strip poker?"
to my mom when I was eight because I thought it was a game,
       not a way to get naked, and was ready to put on
lots of layers that hot July evening—
       p.j.s, raincoat, my patrolboy's belt
with the badge I was so proud of—and figuring
       my mom would do the same with her clothes:

       the cotton dresses she taught fifth grade in
over the jeans and boots she wore for gardening
       and, on top of everything, the long coat she wore
when she went out with my dad on cool nights
       and the ratty mink stole her rich sister had given her.
My dad looked up from his newspaper, looked down again.
       My mother looked up from her book, looked down again,
looked up again, said, "No, thank you, darling,"
       which is how it was in our house:

       no yelling, no explanation, even,
just the assumption that you were a smart kid,
       you could figure things out on your own,
like "No, thanks" meant "no, but thank you anyway"
       and not "zero thanks," or that the K-9 corps
was so-called because K-9 = canine,
       i.e., wasn't just some arbitrary government code—
which is good, I guess, because if people
       aren't constantly explaining stuff to you

       when you're a kid, then you grow up mentally active,
though also doubting everything,
       even yourself, because if you're the one
who comes up with the answers,
       then what the hell good are they?

Which is the kind of thing that led
    Kafka to ask, "What have I in common
with the Jews? I have hardly anything
    in common with myself"

    and might have led Stalin to ask,
"What have I in common with other human beings?"
    only he was too busy coming up with rules
such as this one for the Union of Soviet Composers:
    "The main attention of the Soviet composer
must be directed toward
    the victorious progressive principles
of reality, toward all that is
    heroic, bright, and beautiful."

    But what about all
that is cowardly, dull, and ugly?
    Tightrope-walker Karl Wallenda:
"To be on the wire is life;
    the rest is waiting,"
only there's much more waiting than wire-walking,
    so what are we supposed to do when we're on the ground?
Someone, not Henry James, I think, but one of those
    Henry James kind of guys—cultured, reticent,

    well-off but not too—said a gentleman
was a person who never knowingly made
    anyone else uncomfortable, which is a good idea,
although one you can take too far,
    because one of those smart old Greeks, maybe Sophocles,
said it was better never to be born,
    and think how comfortable that would make everybody,
because if you weren't born, you couldn't bother anyone,
    especially yourself!

    "Are you a runner, Mr. Kirby?" asks Melba
the blood-bank nurse, who has two fingers
    on my right wrist and one eye on her watch

and the other on me, who says,

       no, he's not a runner, though he does a lot
of yard work, and why does she want to know,

       and Melba says, "Because you have a pulse of 50,
and if you have a pulse of 50 and you're not a runner,

       often that means you're dead,"

       which, sooner or later,
I will be, will be naked again, sans p.j.s,

       raincoat, belt and badge, everything.
The blood leaps from a vein in my elbow,

       pools in a plastic sack, and I'm a little whiter
than I was when I read that Ava Gardner said,

       "Deep down, I'm pretty superficial"—
deep down, Ava darling, we're all pretty superficial,

       and beautiful, too, in or out of our clothes.

The House on Boulevard St.

In the days after my first marriage collapsed, I thought
Virtue is gone, in the words of old Sir John Mandeville,
the Clergie is in error, the Devil reigneth, Simonie beareth sway,
Suicide carrieth off many, and Drink taketh the rest,
one of whom was me—I was sleeping single
and drinking doubles, oh yeah, for I didn't have a clue about love,

not one, only the rueful example of my parents
and my pre-teen foray into the world of beefcake magazines,
of *Grecian Guild Pictorial, MANual,* and *Trim*
with their smiling sailors face down on beachtowels,
their Italian teenagers in posing pouches leaning against
fake Roman walls, their latter-day Houdinis in baby oil and chains:

I wanted to *be* one of those guys, not embrace them,
for I knew that even once around the capstan
with those gladiators or jolly jack tars
would not have been right for me, and so
I hoisted barbells I'd made of broomsticks and paint cans
and chinned my spindly frame on our sagging barn door.

As for learning from my peers, well! There was Melvin,
who'd fallen in love with a girl at camp when he was 14
and written her a letter he'd signed "Screwingly yours, Melvin,"
which her mother intercepted and sent to *his* mother,
and Melvin, guessing correctly that letter's contents
from the return address of the envelope, opened same

and tore the incriminating missive to bits,
in which act he was espied by his father, a rabbi, no less,
who visited upon him both the wrath of Yahweh and a roll
of Scotch tape, making Melvin bring together what
he had put asunder, the salacious jigsaw puzzle reassembling itself
as the "scre" sought the "w," the "el" its "vin."

I grew up—what choice did I have?—
         and saw before me the examples of literature,
of Elias Canetti, Nobel-laureate lover of Iris Murdoch
                    who came already equipped with a mistress
and a one-armed wife and was so well-known a sadist
         it was suggested he himself had bitten off his wife's arm. . . .

Then came marriage, betrayal, self-betrayal:
         none of this seemed to me very much like
the golden world of *As You Like It*
                    where gentlefolk fleet time carelessly!
It wasn't *le crépuscule des dieux,* no sir;
         it was more like the gods hadn't even been born yet.

Still, I was hopeful—what choice did I have?—
         because I just knew that, somewhere out there on the veldt,
a beautiful woman was grazing, and one day she'd be mine,
                    though when finally I saw her against the horizon,
it turned out she was neither antelope nor gnu,
         no hartebeest or wildebeest at all but more like a little fox,

a woodland creature with a little pointed nose
         and little pretty whiskers and four dainty silver paws
she'd trot down the sidewalk on, and so pretty and foxy
                    was she that every guy in town who wasn't already
afraid of his current girlfriend followed her around
         with his tongue hanging out like a dog.

And in those days, she lived in a house by the cemetery,
         and when she walked home at night,
dead motherfuckers used to crawl up out of the earth
                    and go rattling after her. And Ted Bundy was living
just a block away, and I bet he stood there dreaming
         about all the women he'd torn to pieces,

and then he hears something pitpatting
         down the sidewalk, and the blood rises behind his teeth,

but when he sees her, he thinks "Christ, a fox . . . , "
               and by now even the ghouls love her so much
they link their bony arms and make a ring around her as she trots along
       because they know Death is there in the shadows.

I was so depressed then that I used to sit around
       and play Elvis Costello's "Allison"
over and over and feel all the emotions I had felt before plus
              a bunch of new ones the old ones had given birth to,
and that house by the cemetery was on
       what was then known as Boulevard St.,

so named, in the uncertain orthography of city signmakers,
       for Simón Bolívar, a.k.a. El Libertador
and "The George Washington of South America"
              for his dogged campaign against the Spanish
that won independence for Bolivia, Panama,
       Colombia, Ecuador, Venezuela, and Peru.

I was also reading the great Marina Tsvetaeva
       who wrote there was no approach to art,
that it was instead a kind of seizing,
              and I thought, why *shouldn't* life imitate books?
Why *shouldn't* I just reach out
       and take what had already taken me?

For I was like a hiker in the mouth of a bear:
       one minute he's writing the species
of a new bird in his journal
              or gulping a swig of designer water
and the next he's being borne off to a cave,
       the hungry cubs batting playfully at his hairless calves,

so at last I just asked her out, and she said yes!
       and at the end of the evening, I asked her again,
and again she said yes! and my heart spun in my chest
              like the Sufi poem that says, "O Sun of Tabriz,
I am so tipsy here in this world,
       I have no tale to tell but tipsiness and rapture!"

To this day, though, that Elvis Costello song makes me want to cry.
   And then I get my Bolívar on
and I wave my sword in the air
               and cut and thrust at the Spain of my self-pity!
Today Boulevard St. is Martin Luther King Blvd.
   and thus honors two great liberators, one secretly.

Per correr miglior acque alza le vele
    omai la navicella del mio ingegno,
    che lascia dietro a sé mar sì crudele;
e canterò di quel secondo regno
    dove l'umano spirito si purga
    e di salire al ciel diventa degno.

To sail over better waters the little boat
    of my wit now hoists her sails,
    leaving behind her a sea so cruel,
and so I'll sing of that second realm
    where our human spirit is buffed up
    and made worthy of rising to Heaven.

—*Il Purgatorio*, Canto I, 1–6

Heat Lightning

The cab pulls up in front of our new apartment
on the Ile Saint-Louis to the unmistakable sounds
        of the *rite amoureux* filling the courtyard,
the woman crying, "Uh, uh, uh, ah oui, AH OUI, AH OUI!"
    as I try to count out the money to the taxi driver

and go, "Okay, ninety, a hundred, a hundred, dammit,"
and him going, "Just start over," and me going, "Eighty,
        eighty-five, uh, eighty, eighty-five,"
and the driver finally waving me off impatiently
    and taking the bills out of my hands one at a time

and holding them up, saying, "See, a hundred francs.
And ten for a tip, okay?" and me saying "Okay!" to him
        and then, to Barbara as we drag the suitcases
up the stairs, "Did you hear that woman having
    that huge orgasm?" and Barbara saying, "Or faking it."

In the months that we lived in that apartment
we were never even sure who the Ah Oui Girl was,
        though we narrowed down the list
of candidates to this one sort of blondish person
    in her twenties who usually looked seriously

out of sorts, figuring surely anybody that grumpy
has the ability to turn on a dime and become
        une vraie tigresse, as I once heard a guy
on the *métro* describe his own girlfriend.
    But mainly we were having one terrific time in Paris:

so many fabulous restaurants! We didn't know
what everything was, yet we ate it anyway, all of it,
        from *aiguillette* and *bourride*
to *loup au fenouil* and *méchoui* to *potiron* and *sandre*
    and *tourteaux*, grilledbroiledboiledroastedfried.

And that was before cheese and dessert.
And opera and dance and concerts and plays—
    we saw Racine's *Phèdre* three times, in fact,
once in English and once as a one-man show and then again
   with a full cast, only in French this time.

   The best part about being in Paris, though,
is that I could spend all this time with Barbara,
    walking along and talking or just sitting
at a little table over an *armagnac* or a coffee
   and saying nothing, and we went out every night,

   and sometimes, as we crossed the courtyard on our way
back in, we'd hear the Ah Oui Girl—that was
    Barbara's name for her, the Ah Oui Girl—
and her boyfriend going at it,
   and often in the last days of summer

   there were flashes of what some people call
heat lightning, which is just other people's real lightning:
    we see it, but it's so far away
that we can't hear the thunder, and we turn our palm up,
   but we can't feel the rain,

   yet it's so hot out there, so we tell ourselves
the lightning is caused by the heat, i.e., by something
    it isn't caused by at all.
One night we came in and these huge bolts were flashing
   silently high over the ancient crenellations

   and cries of "ah oui, ah oui, AH OUI!"
were bouncing off the courtyard walls;
    we'd had maybe a little too much
to drink, and as we headed toward our staircase,
   Barbara said, "They're going at it again!"

   just a little too loudly, and they stopped for a moment,
but by the time we got upstairs,

they'd started afresh, and we opened the windows
and listened to them for a while—
        listened to her, I mean—and then made love ourselves.

        Quietly, though. I would have been embarrassed
for either of us to make noise like the Ah Oui Girl,
                though I envied her enthusiasm
and wished I could relax and just let myself go more
        and not be so, uh, obsessive about everything.

        I wanted to be more like her, even though
I didn't know who she was—I mean, I knew who she was
                when I could hear her, but only then.
Once Barbara suggested that since we'd never identified her
        conclusively, maybe she didn't exist,

        that maybe her boyfriend was an Ah Oui Guy,
a countertenor who did her voice so that everyone
                would think he was a great lover, a kind of fourth-
arrondissement Norman Bates with sex on his mind,
        not stabbing Janet Leigh to death.

        Another reason I was glad to be in Paris
was that at last I was able to read as much
                as I wanted to, and Barbara, too,
and since I was intensely interested in a woman
        both bookish and beautiful and saw reading

        as one more connection to her, in fact, saw it
as indispensable to love, I wondered if the Ah Oui Girl
                was bookish as well or if she and her boyfriend
went at it with sheer animal passion, if theirs was just
        pure screaming brainless hormonal wall-socket sex,

        and one chilly night just before we leave I take a walk
and come in to the sounds of the Ah Oui Girl having
                her usual carefree good time, and Barbara says,
"Did you hear the Ah Oui Girl and her boyfriend?"
        and as I get in bed I say, "I heard the Ah Oui Girl,"

and the next thing I know, the sun is coming up
and I'm going out to get the mail, and when I turn around,
            I bump into somebody and say *Pardon,*
and it's the Ah Oui Girl, and I say *Bonjour, mademoiselle,*
            and she scowls, and I think, Um, maybe that's not her.

Roman Polanski's Cookies

One night I come back from the library late
       and there are all these floodlights
on the Quai de Bourbon, where we live, and there is
           this big table with all these cookies on it
and these big bottles of mineral water,

so I ask somebody what's going on, and he tells me
       Roman Polanski is shooting a scene from a new movie
of his called *The Ninth Gate,* so I hang around
           for a while and soon Roman Polanski shows up,
and he has this monster cigar in his face,

and it sure doesn't look like a King Edward!
       But then I notice that there are these
chocolate-covered graham crackers
           on the cookie table that look like the ones
I used to love when I was a kid, and even though the cookies

are obviously for the actors, I couldn't help sneaking one,
       and it turns out to be exactly the cookie
I'm thinking of, and since by this time the actors
           have shown up and are rehearsing their scene
and showing no interest whatsoever in the cookies,

I take another and another, and soon I'm hog-facing
       those cookies like nobody's business, only
just then I look up, and there's Roman Polanski
           standing there with that big cigar in his hand
and staring at me with a look of pure hatred, as if to say,

"Stop eating all those goddamned chocolate-covered
       graham crackers!" And while part of me
wants to say, Make your movie, dude, it's only a cookie,
           another part of me realizes that maybe they're
his favorite cookies, too, and that even while

My Dead Dad

Our Rue Albert apartment has this pre-Napoleonic water heater
       that lurches to life with a horripilating bang
when, for example, Barbara is taking a bath, as she is now,
       and every time she turns the handle for
more hot water, the heater hesitates a second, then ka-pow!

as though there's a little service technician sitting inside
       working a crossword, his elbows on his knees,
and suddenly he gets the more-hot-water signal and jumps up
       off his little dollhouse chair and runs down
the walkway and throws a shovelful of coal in the furnace

and then walks back, wiping his brow, only to have Barbara
       crank that faucet again, and thwack! he's off
and running while I'm sitting in our French living room
       reading *Journey to the End of Night* by Céline,
whose prose is sweaty and overheated in the first place,

when boom! there he goes once more, sprinting toward
       the furnace, and Barbara is giving
these little cries of either pleasure or surprise or both,
       as she does when bathing, and ba-boom!
there he goes. I imagine him in neatly pressed khakis

and a shirt to match and a hat with a patent-leather brim,
       in the manner of the gas-station attendants
I remember from the days of my youth, and I wonder if he
       is not a relative of the equally little man
in the refrigerator whose job it was, according to my dad,

to turn the light on whenever anyone opened the refrigerator
       door and off when they closed it
and who, in my child's mind, bore a striking resemblance
       to my dad not only in appearance
but also in patience and love of word games and other nonsense.

And if there is such a little man in my French refrigerator
            and water heater and one
in my refrigerator and water heater back home,
            and if there are 5 billion of
us big people in the world, there must be 20 billion of them!

I think, like us, they'd have entertainments, such as
            circuses, barbecues, and *thés dansants,*
but also wars and horrible acts of cruelty!
            Though when peace returned, entire towns of
little people would finish the evening meal and then go on

the *passeggiata* the way the Italians do, the young flirting,
            the old sighing as they admire and envy the young,
the children and dogs getting mixed up in everybody's legs
            as they stroll and chat and ready themselves for
sleep as the clock in the little clock tower strikes eleven,

twelve, one, and the moon comes up—the moon! Which also
            has its little men, according to my dad,
though these are green and, to our eyes, largely invisible,
            since they live on the dark half,
though every once in a while they, too, become curious,

and a few will sneak over into the glary, sunlit side,
            so that when the moon is full, he said,
we should stare at it with every optical instrument at our
            disposal, because if we do, we just might see
one of those little fellows nibbling the piece of cheese

he holds in one hand as he shields his eyes with the other
            and squints down at us. And I haven't even got
to the good little people who live inside each bad one
            of us, according to pop psychologists,
though I don't think my dead dad would have bought that one,

yet since the few people left who knew us both often say
            how much I remind them of him, then I think

if my dead dad lives anywhere at all, he lives inside me.
        Well, and my brother, too, if not
our mother, though there's nothing unusual about that,

because the older I get, the more widows I know, and
        none of them ever says anything about
her dead husband, suggesting perhaps these champions
        weren't so fabulous after all, at least
to them. Sad thought, isn't it, that these men should live

only in the minds of their children. Or maybe my dead dad's
        on the moon, since the alternative point
of view to my smug phenomenological one is that people
        go to heaven when they die,
and heaven's in the sky, and the moon's in the sky,

so who's to say that's not my dead dad up there, his mouth
        full of Limburger or provolone,
shielding his eyes as he tries to find the house
        where we used to live, but he can't,
because it's been torn down, though he'd have no way

of knowing that, so he looks for my mother, and she's there,
        but she lives in a retirement community now,
and he can't believe how old she is, and he's shocked that
        she's as beautiful as he always knew
her to be, only she can't walk now, can't hear, can't see.

And he looks for my brother in Ohio, and he's there,
        and me in Florida, where he left me,
but I'm not there anymore. Hey, Dad! Over here! In France!
        No, France! Great country! Great cheese.
I wish I could take you in my pocket with me everywhere I go.

On My Mother's Blindness

Ninety-five and blind, my mother is doing
her fabulous imitation of Cousin Rack
        sobbing in the back of the church
as his estranged daughter gets married,
        Cousin Rack being this abusive drunk

famous already in my family for two other stories,
        the first involving his attempt to run down
these swans in his powerboat and hitting a stump
        and having to swim to shore, his beautiful craft
heading for the bottom as the swans look on serenely,

        and the second being the time he chased
his mother-in-law, Aunt Gin, around the sofa
        with the butcher knife, too drunk to catch her,
which at least some in the family seem to regret,
        though neither of these tales appeals to my mom

as much as the one she is telling now
        of the exiled Rack, banned from all gatherings,
living alone in well-heeled alcoholic squalor,
        and creeping into the church to see
his only daughter given away by her granddad,

        Uncle Dick, Aunt Gin's husband, and then losing it,
his red face turning crimson as he throws back
        his head and goes—and here my mother twists
her face up like his—"uh-hoo-hoo-HOO-HOO-HOO!!"
        How happy she is! How malicious! How she enjoys

her own malice, and the rest of us, too,
        for she *will* see Cousin Rack's well-earned misery,
will make us see it, too. How I love her
        when I think how much of my childhood I spent
in bed, reading and glancing down the hall

to the kitchen where I'd see her cooking
or marking her students' papers or just
          sitting at the table thinking—about what?
My brother, maybe, and the gloom that grew
          in him until, one day, it suddenly vanished forever.

Or my father and his cooling love. Or me:
          if I'd been a mail-order child, there were
so many things wrong with me—asthma, allergies,
          polio, chronic self-pity persisting to this day—
that another mother would have sent me back.

          My mother is the best storyteller I know,
and I thought of her in Paris when I read
          that the great French poet Jacques Prévert
saw this beggar who had a sign that said,
          "Blind Man Without a Pension,"

and when he asked the beggar how he was doing,
          the beggar said, "Oh, very badly. People just
pass by and drop nothing in my hat, the swine,"
          so Prévert said, "Here, give me that placard,"
and, passing by a few days later, asked again

          how things were going, and the beggar
said, "Fantastic! My hat fills up
          three times a day," and that was because,
on the back of his placard, Prévert had written,
          "Spring is coming, but I won't see it."

My mother is her own great French poet.
          Rack's tears leap from her sightless face
as she tells her story—though when he was found dead
          and so covered with mold "at first they thought
he was a black man," I remember her weeping.

The Search for Baby Combover

In Paris one night the doorbell rings,
        and there's this little guy, shaking like a leaf
and going "uh-uh-uh-UNH-ah!" and his eyes get big
        and he raises his hands like a gospel singer
and goes "UNH-ah-uh-uh-uh-UNH-uh-ah!"

and for just a fraction of a second I think
        he's doing the first part of Wilson Pickett's
"Land of a Thousand Dances" and that he wants me
        to join him in some kind of weird welcome
to the neighborhood, so I raise my hands a little

and begin to sort of hum along, though
        not very loudly in case I'm wrong about this,
and I'm smiling the way old people smile
        when they can't hear you but want you to know
that everything's okay as far as they're concerned

or a poet smiles in a roomful of scientists,
        as if to say, "Hey! I'm just a poet!
But your stuff's great, really! Even if
        I don't understand any of it!" And by the time
I start to half-wonder if this gentleman wants me

to take the you-got-to-know-how-to-pony part
        or means to launch into it himself, he gives
a little hop and slaps his hands down to his sides
        and says, "PLEASE! YOU MUST NOT MOVE
THE FURNITURE AFTER ELEVEN O'CLOCK OF THE NIGHT!"

so I lower my own hands and say, "Whaaaa . . . ?"
        and he says, "ALWAYS YOU ARE MOVING IT WHEN
THE BABY TRY TO SLEEP! YOU MUST NOT DO IT!"
        And now that he's feeling a little bolder,
he steps in closer, where the light's better,

and I see he's got something on his head,
        like strands of oily seaweed, something
you'd expect to find on a rock after one of
            those big tanker spills in the Channel,
so I lean a little bit and realize it's what

stylists call a "combover," not a bad idea
        on the tall fellows but definitely a grooming no-no
for your vertically challenged caballeros,
           of which Monsieur here is certainly one,
especially if they are yelling at you.

But I'd read an article about AA that said
        when your loved ones stage an intervention
and go off on you for getting drunk
           and busting up the furniture and running out
into traffic and threatening to kill the President,

it's better to just let them wind down
        and then say, "You're probably right,"
because if you're combative, they will be, too,
        and then your problems will just start over again,
so I wait till Mr. Combover stops shaking—

it's not nice, I know, but it's the first name that comes to mind—
        and I say, "You're probably right," and he raises
a finger and opens his mouth as if to say something
           but then snaps his jaw shut and whirls around
and marches downstairs, skidding a little

and windmilling his arms and almost falling
        but catching himself, though not without
that indignant backward glance we all give
           the stupid step that some stupid idiot would have
attended to long ago if he hadn't been so stupid.

The next day, I ask Nadine the *gardienne*
        qu'est-ce que c'est the deal *avec* the *monsieur*

qui lives under *moi,* and Nadine says his *femme*
    is *toujours* busting his chops, but *il est* afraid
of her, so *il* takes out his *rage* on the rest of *nous.*

There's something else, though: a few days later,
    Barbara and I see Mr. and Mrs. Combover
crossing the Pont Marie, and she is a virtual giantess
      compared to him! Now I remember once hearing Barbara
give boyfriend advice to this niece of mine,

and Barbara said (1) he's got to have a job,
    (2) he's got to tell you you're beautiful all the time,
and (3) he's got to be taller than you are,
      so when I see Mrs. Combover looming over her hubby,
I think, Well, that explains the busted chops.

Not only that, Mrs. Combover looks cheap.
    She looks rich, sure—Nadine had told me *Monsieur*
is some *sorte de* diplomat *avec* the Chilean delegation—
      but also like one of those professional ladies
offering her services up around the Rue St. Denis.

But who are they, really? "Combover" is one
    of those names from a fifties black-and-white movie;
he's the kind of guy neighborhood kids call "Mr. C."
      and who has a boss who says things like, "Now see here,
Combover, this sort of thing just won't do!"

He's like one of Dagwood's unnamed colleagues—
    he's not even Dagwood, who at least excites
Mr. Dithers enough to be fired a couple
      of times a week, not to mention severely beaten.
Only Dagwood is really in charge. Everything goes his way!

Despite chronic incompetence, ol' Dag keeps
    the job that allows him his fabulous home life:
long naps, towering sandwiches, affectionate
      and well-behaved teenaged children, a loyal dog,
and, best of all, the love of Blondie.

Blondie! The name says it all: glamorous but fun.
        Big trashy Mrs. Combover is not glamorous,
although she thinks she is, and no fun at all.
                She is the anti-Blondie. Her job seems to be
to stay home and smoke, since we're always smelling

the cigarette fumes that seep up through the floor
        into our apartment day and night. And he says
we're keeping Baby Combover awake when we move
                the furniture, which we've never done, but then
we've never seen Baby Combover, either. Or heard him.

Baby Combover: the world's first silent baby.
        Barbara has this theory that, after a life
of prostitution, Mrs. Combover has not only repented but
                undergone a false pregnancy and imaginary birth.
Therefore, the reason why Baby Combover is silent

is that he is not a real baby who fusses and eats and
        wets and poops but is instead a pillowcase with knots
for ears and a smiley face drawn with a Magic Marker and
                a hole for its mouth so Mrs. Combover can teach it
to smoke when it's older, like eight, say.

Now I know what they fight about: "You never spend
        any time with the baby!" hisses Mrs. Combover.
"I will—later, when he can talk!" says Mr. Combover.
                "Here I am stuck with this baby all day long!
And those horrible people upstairs!"

And he says, "Oh, be silent, you . . . prostitute!"
        And she says, "Quiet, you horrible man—
not in front of the baby!" Maybe it's time
                for a call to the police. Or the newspapers.
I can see the headlines now: OU EST L'ENFANT COMBOVER?

I feel sorry for him. With parents like these,
        it would be better if someone were to kidnap him.

Or I could take him back to America with me,
                    I who have a wife who loves me and two grown sons.
Why not? We've got all this extra room now.

We'll feed him a lot and tickle him;
                    there's nothing funnier than a fat, happy baby.
And when the boys come home to visit,
                    they'll take him out with them in their sports cars:
"It's my little brother!" they'll say. "He's French!"

The neighborhood kids, once a band of sullen mendicants,
                    will beg us to let him play with them,
even though he doesn't speak their language.
                    Look! There they go toward the baseball field,
with Baby Combover under their arm!

I love you, Baby Combover! You *are* Joseph Campbell's
                    classic mythical hero, i.e., "an agent of change
who relinquishes self-interest and breaks down
                    the established social order." But you're so pale!
You've stayed out too long and caught cold.

Barbara and the boys gather around his bed;
                    they hug each other, and we try not to cry.
Baby Combover is smiling—he always smiled, that kid.
                    His little mouth begins to move, and we lean in
and think we hear him say, "Be bwave fo' me. . . ."

Back in Paris, Mr. Combover grows a full head of hair.
                    Mrs. Combover reaches up to touch it.
He puts down his attaché case and caresses her cheek.
                    "How beautiful you are!" he says. It's so quiet now.
Then they hear it: in the next room, a child is crying.

The Elephant of the Sea

Because I make the big bucks fooling around
with words, in France sometimes I like to say
        "Sylvia Plath" instead of "*s'il vous plaît*,"
as when I open the door for Barbara and say,
        "*Après-vous*, Sylvia Plath!" But yesterday
the lady in the *boulangerie* asked me what I wanted,
        and I said, "*Une baguette*, Sylvia Plath! Crap. . . ."

Before I move to France, I have to help
my friend from France buy his first American automobile,
        and naturally he wants everything on his car
to be just like mine, right down to the manatee on the tag,
        for which I pay an extra seventeen dollars that
goes into some kind of special fund for endangered species.
        He says, "You have zuh elephant of zuh sea

on your matriculation?" Tag, I say, tag!
And manatee! which is a Native American word meaning, uh,
        l'éléphant de mer, and no, you don't want it,
because we're trying to save money here, remember?
        We go over this several times, yet when we are in
the tag office and I am filling out a form to have his title
        sent to my address, I hear Antoine say,

"I can have zuh elephant of zuh sea
on my matriculation?" to a clerk who's got this grin
        on her face like she's either seeing God
or having an aneurysm, and I can see she loves it,
        she's going to tell the women she goes fishing with
on Lake Jackson about this foreign fellow,
        nice as he could be, though, who comes into

the office the other day and says, "elephant of
zuh sea" and "matriculation," and they'll say,
        "Wanda, hush! You're scaring the bass!"
and so she'll tell her husband, who will say,

"Uh-huh! Any more of these potatoes?"
and also everyone at her fortieth class reunion
       and her grandchildren and their children, too,

       and they'll ignore her as well, the little ones
thinking, Whoa, G-momma's telling those old stories again!
       And on her last day, Pastor Blair will be there
saying, "That's all right, now, Wanda, you just let go,
       you hear?" And she'll wheeze and say,
"And then this fellow says, 'I can have zuh elephant
       of zuh sea'—ah, glory!"

       Up to this point in his life, Pastor Blair
will have had about him the same "divine stupidity"
       that Tennyson attributed to Garibaldi,
but the phrase "zuh elephant of zuh sea" will wake him
       right up, it'll hit him like a triple espresso,
and he'll always remember it, though he'll change
       the details as he works them into a story of his own

       about this dying member of his congregation
who raved about this particular foreign individual who,
       etc., and so forth and so on in endless retellings
which are in turn picked up by others who incorporate them
       into their stories until finally "zuh elephant
of zuh sea"—well, it won't be like France at all, will it,
       it'll be like Deutschland, i.e., *über alles*.

       And the baker, she'll say to her husband,
"Funniest thing: today this stuttering spastic hillbilly
       zombie hayseed-type dude calls me 'Sylvia Plath,'"
and her husband says, "You mean S'il Vous Plaît,
       the author of *The Colossus* (1960) and *Ariel* (1965)?"
and she'll pop herself on the forehead with a floury hand
       and say, "You know the dates?"

A Fine Frenzy

   She tells me, "It smells like your mother"
as we enter room 53 (twin beds, bath, 95 euros)
            of the Hôtel Jeanne d'Arc in Paris, and it's true,
      there's a heavy though not displeasing scent
of lilac face powder of the kind used
            by old Southern ladies of a certain generation.
On the flight over, I'd read her the section
      of *Pantagruel* in which Panurge tells a great Parisian

      lady he'd like to show her Master John Thursday,
"a sprightly fellow . . . who will play you a jig
            that you'll feel in the very marrow of your bones"
      and who is "so good at finding all the cracks
and quirks and special spots in the carnal trap
            that after him there is no need of a broom,"
only how do you show someone Master John Thursday
      in a room that smells like your mother?

      In the museums, we see many odalisques
in the tradition of Raphael and Titian and Canova
            and Manet and Ingres, not to mention quite a few
statues of the type that were supposed to have
      so deceived poor John Ruskin that it was
            a marriage-ending shock to him when he saw his wife
naked on their wedding night and realized real women
      aren't all sleek and hairless, um, down there.

      But the course of true love never did run smooth,
did it, reader? I mean, there's always something,
            for just as there are kisses, cuddles, endearments,
peonies, mums, long-stemmed roses, chocolate bars,
      and gourmet meals followed by raisings, lowerings,
            unsnappings, and gasps of surprise, so, too,
are there wens, buboes, sties, fat rolls that appear overnight,
      hacking coughs, smart remarks, receipts for gifts

he or she bought that you didn't get, slaps,
raised middle fingers, cuss words, gasps of surprise.
Now I know Ruskin never hung around
locker rooms, never played power forward for
the United Crowned Heads of Europe
Regional High School Fightin' Colonizers
("Think the Colonizers stand a chance of making it
to the finals this year, Mike?" "Sure do, Bill,

and there's the whistle as John Ruskin passes off
to King Leopold of Belgium, who drives for the basket,
pausing on the way to occupy the Congo and enslave
the populace and grab the wealth for himself
and his buddies and destabilize the entire region
for a century or more . . . "), but you'd think
he might have glanced down at his own arrangement
once or twice and concluded that women have something

similar. Because if he had, and if he'd played his cards
right, I bet Mrs. Ruskin would have scrubbed his face
nightly with her little washcloth there! Ha, ha!
Or at least not threatened to summon her servants
and kinsmen and have his arms and legs cut off,
as the great lady of Paris did to Panurge,
though, come to think of it, Ruskin might have liked that,
might have gone for precisely that sort of hullaballoo,

the stones of his big-ass ideological fortress in disarray
at his feet along with his step-ins and her culottes, the flag lowered,
the drawbridge down, the moat full of skinnydippers.
Ah, men. Ah, women. Ah, love, lust, arousal,
desire, concupiscence, Cupidism, curds and whey—
how delicious are these and many other
of life's tidbits, poetry included, though more than one of them
is as rough as a nutmeg grater, rough as a bear.

Seventeen Ways from Tuesday

At the Miró exhibit in the Centre Pompidou,
      I hear a guy say to his girlfriend, "When we get back to the hotel,
            I'm going to put it to you seventeen ways from Tuesday,"
and I think, now what does that mean, exactly?
            I know what "it" is, but why that number and that day?
      Also, what is it about art that makes people so happy?
It's probably seventeen because that's a funny number,

as the comedians will tell you: one through six aren't,
      seven through twelve are, thirteen through sixteen
            are duds, and anything from seventeen on is funny again.
And when you're trying to get sexy with somebody,
            it's probably a good idea to suggest, not slapstick
      or parody or satire and certainly not farce, travesty,
caricature, burlesque, *opera buffa,* buffoonery, miming,

squibbing, lampooning, or hudibrastics—
      especially not hudibrastics—but, instead, good humor,
            or, better, a good nature, i.e., a tender one.
As for the day, that's easy: you rest on Sunday, you take care of
            the first part of the week's work on Monday
      so you can start thinking about your fun from Tuesday forward,
and now there are only four days left for that,

but you being you, you won't offer that special someone
      you share all your fun with a mere four choices
            but the square of four plus one.
Now about art: art makes people happy because—
            well, let's see what Miró has to say on the subject.
      This is from a 1936 interview with Georges Duthuit
in *Cahiers d'Art:* "Painting and poetry are done

in the same way you make love; it's an exchange
      of blood, a total embrace—without caution,
            without any thought of protecting yourself."
Hmm. You're right, reader: that does sound pretty stupid!

Ha, ha! Tell you what, Joan:
    you hang on to your day job there! To put it another way,
you leave the inkpots alone, and I won't start

splattering the canvases! I think art makes people happy
        because it makes them feel like children again,
                spoiled children: even though we're tiny and penniless
and half their size, the grownups are doing everything they can
            to please us—look, here's a roomful of paintings,
        a two-and-a-half-hour movie, a book as thick as a mid-sized city's
telephone directory, and there's more on the way!

Later I see the young lovers in the museum cafeteria,
        and they seem broodish, distant from one another.
                I wonder if he has followed up on his original
playful proposition with something less playful
                and more manlike, i.e., doggy. If so, then
        he should make short work of his *blanquette de veau*
avec sauce béchamel and maybe reach over and finish off

the *coq au Riesling* she has barely touched and coax her
            into returning with him to the exhibit, for Miró at his best,
                that is, when painting, not writing, is childlike,
fastening wire or feathers to paper and connecting them
                into busy little villages with a single free-hand line
        or daubing in great balloons of color that threaten
to burst from the frame or concocting entire universes

of bugs and dunce caps and ying-yang symbols
        and leering pollywogs and big nameless buttocky doodads
                that seem to be part of a strange dream, yeah,
but a fun dream, not a disturbing one,
                and even when he is painting figuratively
        (yes, he did that, too), he produces, not
a conventional portrait *à la* Degas or even the young Picasso,

but one of a thick-haired guy in weird Catalonian p.j.s
        leaning up against a Japanese print,

the whole set against a background of yellow
as bright as egg yolk or gold or the sun itself.
　　　　Lovers, be like painters, i.e., playful, not grim.
　　　Painters, you be like painters, too! Leave the writing to us.
And you know what to do already, poets, so get busy.

The Exorcist of Notre-Dame

Just after we get to Paris I learn that there's an exorcist
        at Notre-Dame named Père Nicolas, and when I stop by,
sure enough, there he is with his name tag on,
                a chubby white-haired guy talking to an elderly lady
who doesn't look at all as though she thinks

the Seine is filled with blood or the College of Cardinals
        is a bunch of scaly Komodo dragons flicking their tongues
around and electing Beelzebub pope, and while I'd like to
                hang out and watch the people to see if the ones
with demons turn their heads around backward and say,

"Yugga-ugga-mooga-waaga-aaga!" when they walk by
        or if their T-shirts begin to writhe as though a couple
of rattlesnakes are having seizures just before Père Nicolas
                jumps up to put the double whammy woo-woo juju on them,
I need to get home so we can make an 8:30 booking

at the Square Trousseau, and in the restaurant there's a youngish woman
        sitting next to us with an older guy
who reminds me of my dead father, and they're quiet,
                as father and daughter have a right to be, and he's eating well,
even if he seems a little bored by the whole thing,

a little downcast, though he looks up at me after a while
        and then down again and then up rather sharply,
as though he recognizes me, and a little smile crosses his face
                for just an instant. And there's another table behind ours
with six drunk Brits talking football at the top of their lungs,

though they're so drunk and they have so much food
        in their mouths that they sound like jackals or bears
who've only made it through the first two weeks
                of the human-conversation class: "Ugga-wooga-
agga-hagga-MANCHESTER UNITED!-agga-mugga-

wugga-ARSENAL!-oogga!" So the old guy and his daughter
          get dessert, and Barbara and I our main courses while the Brits
bark and snap at each other, and the old guy keeps looking at me,
                    and when the check arrives, the daughter pays,
and he comes over and says, "Enjoy your meal?" and he sounds the way

my dad would have sounded if my dad had been French,
          and he tilts his head toward the noisy table and says,
"They're a bit noisy, don't you think?"
                    and he's so much like my dad that I feel my jaw
begin to quiver and tears start down my face, and the old guy puts his hand

on my shoulder and says, "Don't cry. I have good news for you,"
          and for a moment I'm convinced that it is my dad,
that he has news for me from the other side, that it's nice over there,
                    always sunny and cool, and you can get anything you want
to eat, and that he's got this great place, it's like a house

in one of those medieval woodcuts that's open to the world,
          with a river on one side and a winding road on the other,
and one day my mother will come up that road,
                    and then my older brother, and then me,
and he tilts his head toward the Brits and says,

"It could be worse," and I'm so ashamed of my tears
          that all I can say is, "H-how?" and he leans a little closer
and jacks his eyebrows a couple of times and says,
          "They could have cell phones," and, well, no, it isn't my dad, is it,
there's probably not even an afterlife at all, is there,

nor demons, or at least no demons other than the ones
          who're there to dog us on the days when exhaustion or fear
has made us allergic to everyone, our own selves included,
                    the days dead opposite to what Randall Jarrell called
"the day of our life," i.e., one with the right lunch, right music

and books and movies, right sweetheart, right friends.
          And I want to talk to Père Nicolas about all this,

but the sign outside his confessional says he speaks
>only German and Spanish and French, not English,
meaning I'd have to talk my strictly intermediate-level French

to him, about which I'm self-conscious enough already,
>not to mention—and I know this sounds stupid, but I've run out
of conditioner and can't find a French kind that works for me,
>so my hair is sticking out all over the place like that of
a "clown" (i.e., not a circus performer but Latin *colonnus*

or rube, clodhopper, mountain William, bumpkin,
>guy on a day pass), and there I'd be going, "*Pensez-vous,*
pensez, um, *c'est-à-dire*, uh, *pensez-vous*," and later that night,
>as the priests are all sitting around the big oak dinner table
working on their *jarret de porc rôti* and their *daube à la provençale*,

the others, the older priests who're jealous or the modern ones
>who don't believe in demonic possession
in the first place, are kidding him and saying, "Run into
>any devils today, Père Nicolas?"
and he says "No, just a woman from Ghana

with stomach pains and a *monsieur* who thinks people
>are talking about him on the *métro*
and, uh, oh yeah! this stuttering sort of spastic hillbilly
>zombie hayseed-type person who, well,
I really don't know what he wanted," and it could play out

that way, all cynical and funny and word-drunk,
>because in his line of work,
Père Nicolas would have to have a sense of humor, wouldn't he,
>or else he'd end up consulting one of the other
94 licensed exorcists in France, though in his secret heart

I know he thinks my dad is right, my dead dad, that is,
>the real one, and that my real dad is up there
in that little house, and my mother and brother will come up
>that road to meet him, and in time, I'll come, too,
not on the road, but on the river, in a little silver boat.

The Desperate Hours

PARIS—M. Baudin, the Minister of Public Works, yesterday narrowly escaped a revolver bullet intended for his colleague of the Foreign Office. He was proceeding to attend the Ministerial Council at the Elysée, when a woman, holding a little boy by the hand, fired a revolver at him. Fortunately no one was hurt. The woman, Countess Olszewska, was arrested and taken before the police commissary for the Madeleine quarter.

—"100 Years Ago Today," *International Herald Tribune,* 6/17/01

I'm wishing *I* had a revolver as I doze and wake sharply
      at graduation and hear a voice say "Adolf . . . Marie . . . Hitler!"
and think about our search for a good restaurant in the little town
         of Port-en-Bessin this summer and how I'm just stepping out
of the car as Barbara hands me this delicious peach

and then I'm walking up the street, wiping the peach juice
      from my chin and looking for a trash can or storm drain
to toss the pit in, but before I can find one, this *monsieur*
         comes out of his establishment and nods to me, so I put my hand
behind my back and ask him about the evening's specials,

and a voice says "Elvis . . . Louise . . . Presley!"
      and I'm thinking, if I had a revolver, I could discharge it
into the air, even though I was so against guns once,
         back when I was a draft counselor, back in the day
of the Kent State incident, when the guardsmen opened fire

on kids just walking to class, and the country was so divided then
      that a poll showed most Ohioans thought the dead college students
"got what they deserved." Several rows ahead, I see
         Professor Mark Pietralunga of the Modern Languages Department
and recall the story he told me about his student days

and the invitation to go backpacking through Greece
      with some Italian youth, and more than one comely maiden
among them, only he has no backpack and sports instead
         a Samsonite Tourister suitcase which he lugs gamely down
country lanes with the merrymakers, joking and singing

and anticipating the night's revels and then taking a shortcut
            across this field and hearing a terrible bellowing and realizing
they are being pursued by one furious Greek bull!
                        And there they go, the lissome Italians shrieking in terror,
and the professor-to-be among them, lurching this way and that

as he passes the suitcase from one hand to the other
            and tries not to end his days as a taurine casualty!
Oh, ha, ha! Bet *he* wished he had a gun then!
                        "Barbra . . . James . . . Streisand!" says the voice—
my god, it's been three hours, will the ceremony *never* end?

I needn't say why, but last week I was in the recovery room
            of the Tallahassee Endoscopy Center, and a half dozen
decent Christian beldames are lying there, the kind of women
                        who carry wicker-basket purses and wear Christmas sweatshirts
with elves and reindeer decoupaged across the bosom,

and I overhear the nurse telling one of these ladies that naturally
            she's going to feel "a little stuffy" after the "procedure"
and she should try to "pass air" and not be embarrassed
                        about doing so, but these ladies aren't about to pass air in front
of other ladies like themselves, much less a strange male,

and I think, that would be good, too, for somebody to cut one
            about now, preferably one of the on-stage dignitaries,
the commencement speaker, maybe, or perhaps
                        the governor himself, a good slow ripper yet one loud enough
for the mike to pick it up so everyone can hear,

when omigod! Professor Karen Berkley, Psychology, is choking
            on a Mento given to her by Professor Bruce Bickley, English!
But then Professor Berkley is pounded on the back vigorously
                        and the offending Mento pops loose and rolls into the aisle!
Whew! No need for a gun, after all, nor the other thing.

When the restaurateur in Port-en-Bessin finishes telling me
            about his shellfish specialties and invites me to come back

that evening to partake of them, he reaches out to shake
                        my hand, and I shake his, and he looks at his palm and then
at me, and I shrug and say "peach pit" in English because at the time

I can't think how to say "peach pit" in French.
                        Aristotle says a thing whose presence or absence
makes no difference to a whole is not part of that whole,
                        so I guess guns aren't all that important to me
or no more important than a *noyau de pêche*.

What was Countess Olszewska thinking as she fired a ball
                        at Monsieur Baudin's unnamed colleague with one hand
while she clutched the fingers of little Pierre or Jacques
                        or Jean-André with the other? She couldn't have known
that a similar act would lead to a war in just 13 years

and that 10 million would die in it just so everyone could
                        rest up for a couple of decades and then enjoy the same carnage
all over again, and clearly she wasn't thinking of what
                        a bad example she was setting for her little man there;
probably she just wanted to have a regular day but also shoot somebody.

As the auditorium empties of professors and grads
                        and justly-proud papas and mamas, I think how,
after Barbara and I had gorged ourselves on the Frenchman's crabs
                        and mussels and oysters, his *marennes* and *fines de claires,*
his *crustacés,* his *bigorneaux* or winkles, we walked down to the docks

to listen to a quartet warble sea chanteys, and one of the musicians
                        played the spoons, and I used to think I was pretty good at spoons,
but this guy made his sound like a harpsichord, doing runs
                        and glissandos and arpeggios, and if I'd had my spoons
with me, I would have thrown them into the Atlantic, and if I'd had a gun,

I'd have thrown it, too. And then part of me would have wanted it back:
                        Bad Dave splashes into the waves and dives for the gun
but then chokes and sputters and cries, "Help, Good Dave!
                        Help, help!" And Good Dave stretches out his hand
toward Bad Dave, their fingers almost meeting, but not quite.

The Little Sisters of the Sacred Heart

I'm bouncing across the Scottish heath in a rented Morris Minor
         and listening to an interview with Rat Scabies, drummer
of the first punk band, The Damned, and Mr. Scabies,
      who's probably 50 or so and living comfortably on royalties,
is as recalcitrant as ever, as full of despair and self-loathing,

but the interviewer won't have it, and he keeps calling him "Rattie,"
         saying, "Ah, Rattie, it's all a bit of a put-on, isn't it?"
and "Ah, you're just pulling the old leg now, aren't you, Rattie?"
      to which Mr. Scabies keeps saying things like
"We're fooked, ya daft prat. Oh, yeah, absolutely—fooked!"

Funny old Rattie—he believed in nothing, which is something.
         If it weren't for summat, there'd be naught, as they say
in that part of the world. I wonder if his dad wasn't a bit of a bastard,
      didn't drink himself to death, say, as opposed to a dad like mine,
who, though also dead now, was as nice as he could be when he was alive.

A month before, I'd been in Florence and walked by the *casa di cura* where
         my son Will was born 27 years ago, though it's not a hospital
now but a home for the old nuns of Le Suore Minime del Sacra Cuore
      who helped to deliver and bathe and care for him when he was just
a few minutes old, and when I look over the gate, I see three

of these holy sisters sitting in the garden there, and I wave at them,
         and they wave back, and I wonder if they were on duty
when Will was born, these women who have had no sex at all,
      probably not even very much candy, yet who believe in something
that may be nothing, after all, though I love them for giving me my boy.

They're dozing and talking, these mystical brides of Christ,
         and thinking about their Husband, and it looks to me
as though they're having their version of the *sacra conversazione*,
      a favorite subject of Renaissance artists in which people who care
for one another are painted chatting together about noble things,

and I'm wondering if, as I walk by later when the shadows are long,
           will their white faces be like stars against their black habits,
the three of them a constellation about to rise into the vault
        that arches over Tuscany, the fires there now twinkling,
now steadfast in the chambered heart of the sky.

Americans in Italy

       As I wait in line to get into Vasari's Corridor,
which stretches from the Palazzo Vecchio to the Pitti Palace
       and along which Cosimo de' Medici could walk without
the bodyguard he employed to keep the thugs of the Albizi
       or the Pazzi families from sticking their knives in him,
I am passed by dozens of my countrymen and -women,
       most of whom are dressed as though they're here
not to look at the Botticellis and the Ghirlandaios
       but to play city-league softball or mow the lawn.

       The three things Americans visiting Italy worry about most
are (1) being cheated (2) being made to eat something
       they don't like, and (3) being cheated in the course
of being made to eat something they don't like.
       To these people, I say: Americans, do not worry.
Italians will not cheat you. Dishonesty requires calculation,
       and Italians are no fonder of calculation than we are.
As for the food, remember that you are in a restaurant,
       for Christ's sake, and therefore it is highly unlikely

       that your handsome, attentive waiter will bring you
a bunch of boiled fish heads, much less a bowl of hairspray soup
       or a slice of tobacco pie topped with booger ice cream.
Indeed, you have already been both cheated and made to eat
       bad food in your so-called Italian restaurant in Dearborn
or Terre Haute where the specialty is limp manicotti
       stuffed with cat food and welded to an oversized ashtray
with industrial-strength tomato sauce; therefore be not
       like the scholar in *The Charterhouse of Parma*

       who never pays for the smallest trifle without looking up
its price in Mrs. Starke's *Travels*, where it states how much
       an Englishman should pay for a turkey, an apple,
a glass of milk, and so on, but eat, drink, and spend freely,
       for tomorrow you will again be in Grand Rapids or Fort Wayne.
As Cosimo strolled his corridor, he could glance out from time to time

to see if three or four of the abovementioned Pazzi or Albizi
were gathering to discuss something that almost certainly
        would not have been a surprise birthday party for him.

        Also, he could literally walk on the heads of his subjects!
Ha, ha! And if he didn't enjoy doing that,
        I can think of plenty of people who would, can't you?
Indeed, there is another type of American who not only
        visits Italy but also writes poems about the place in which
we, the readers, are made to feel like ostlers or bootblacks
        or street sweepers on which they, the lordly, step from
one palace to another, never soiling the hems of their silken gowns
        as they tread unthinkingly on such human cobblestones as we,

        and here I remember what my student Ron Jenkins wrote
about just such a poet who had written just such a poem,
        that is, "As a gay man from desperately poor circumstances,
I get bored—even angry—very easily at the lives
        of literate, affluent, heterosexual bourgeoisie,
especially those with the means to loll around piazzas."
        Ha! Ron, I too hate the fuckers, and I hereby resolve
never to be one. That is, I can't help being literate
        and heterosexual, but I'll never be affluent,

        and, try as I may, I've never been able to loll,
either in the personal or the poetic sense, and it is perhaps
        because of this very physical ungainliness that I also like,
as a sort of frame around one's personal world, not only a *corridoio*
        or corridor but also the *chiostro* or cloister
that's found at the heart of every monastery so the holy fathers
        of this or that order will have a place to walk and praise God
for His generosity in giving them not only soft breezes and flowers
        and birdsong but also their own sins to contemplate,

        as well as a *studiolo,* or—well, there's no one-word translation
for this term meaning "phone-booth-sized reading room
        with elaborate wood inlay and other fine appointments
intended to inspire deep philosophical thought

on the part of a nobleperson, generally a duke,
who repairs there when in need of such rumination."
    Corridoio, chiostro, studiolo: snug spaces,
tiny hidey-holes in a world too big for its own good,
    refuges from the sun or from assassins.

    Why, they are like the shapes of pasta or of little cookies,
some like ears, others like pens or butterflies.
    Mr. Wordsworth said nuns fret not at their narrow cells
nor poets within the confines of their sonnets.
    Though I have to say I was just a tad discomfited
the other day: as I was looking through an iron gate
    at the very pretty Chiostro degli Aranci in the Badia Fiorentina,
a man comes up and stands right behind me—
    as in, not merely close to or near me, but *right behind* me,

    his toes teaching my heels, his breath warm on my neck.
Now who is this guy, you are asking yourself:
    an associate professor of art history? My alter ego? A rogue monk
like the one in *The Marble Faun*? A German?
    And these, of course, are precisely the same questions
I am asking myself! But when I turn to look at him,
    I see he is a Midwesterner, from Dayton or Cleveland, say,
or better yet, from Cincinnati, the only U.S. city
    named for a secret society!

    He is a large, rumpled man
and he smiles at me, though sadly, and I wonder
    if he isn't the kind of guy who, when he gets off work,
dresses up as a clown and goes to cheer up sick kids
    in the hospitals there in the Cincinnati area,
but now he's looking out at the garden with the well
    at its center and he's thinking of his own mortality,
and he knows that, in a few hours,
    the Benedictine monks will be walking around

    this same cloister after dinner and thinking about something
very similar, although in his imagination

he sees them not as monks but as clowns, big solemn guys
with baggy pants and big orange tufts of hair and bright red noses,
    and they clasp their hands behind their backs
and they look at the ground as they shuffle along,
    their size 30 shoes slapping the terrazzo,
and they're thinking, Life's pretty terrible—
    well, no, not really, not when you think about it.

The Laughter of Pigs

After Osvaldo, after the *bocconcini* and the *fior di zucca*,
      we were walking and then we were watching these pigs,
and this one pig wallowed in his slough
              as the others chewed grass and made pig noises,
and then the pig in the slough cut one,
      the bubbles churning the water behind him

like the exhaust of an outboard motor,
      and as we began to walk away,
I looked back at the other pigs to see
              how they'd react, but they did nothing,
didn't nudge each other or roll their eyes,
      and in that moment I thought less of them

as a species and wasn't ashamed that I had eaten
      so many of their brethren.
And the one in the water acted neither boastful
              nor ashamed—the pig was not sheepish.
St. Francis would have called him Brother Pig,
      but to me he was just an animal.

Who are we, anyway? Remember when I bought
      that maul, which is like an ax, only bigger,
and the clerk at Sears said, "Want a bag?"
              And I said no, and I had to get
something else from another store,
      so there I was with this huge tool in my hand,

and parents were pulling their kids to one side,
      even though I had the boys with me.
To the other shoppers, I was a male with a maul in the mall.
              To them, I wasn't a good father about to go home
and spend the afternoon splitting firewood
      with his sons. To them, I wasn't an author of,

not poems in those days, or good poems, at any rate,
      because mainly I was writing reference books then,

93

a few of which were well reviewed, especially in Scotland,
                so that I used to imagine
these stolid Scottish librarians standing around at
                their annual meetings in Edinburgh or Glasgow,

brushing the pipe ash off their kilts and saying,
                "Guid lad, Kirby," and "Ay, that wee chappie."
Though it's been years since I've done anything in that line,
                so maybe now they're saying,
"Whatever happened to the lad?"
                and "It's nae the same since Kirby went missing."

When they grunt, the sound pigs make is very akin
                to laughter. Maybe they *are* laughing, as if to say,
"Look at them silly folk, hanging about
                with nothing better to do than to gawk at we pigs!"
Or, on a somewhat more literary plane,
                "What fools these mortals be!"

Or maybe they don't notice us at all.
                Even if those pigs could have spoken, if, later that day,
a cow or goose had said, "What do you make
                of those people who were watching you today?"
the pigs might reply, "What people?"
                or even, "What are people?"

In the afterworld, what if the gods are pigs?
                What if it is we who are farting in the mud
and pigs who walk by arm in arm,
                commenting on the *oeuvres* of the great pig poets?
Your honors, I was wrong to eat you, after all.
                But you understand, don't you? You tasted so good.

The Beauty Trap

At the interval, I learn that directors of operas like *Lucia*
sometimes go out of their way to avoid "the beauty trap," that is,
a production totally based on sweetness and pleasing effects,
but just then the bell rings, so I hurriedly finish copying
from David Hamilton's *Metropolitan Opera Encyclopedia*

(authoritative, yes, but 35 euros and, what,
3–4 additional pounds in an already hard-to-close carry-on bag)
Joan Sutherland's comment that her only problem
with the role is that she is "beginning to feel a bit silly
playing an eighteen-year-old girl" because "after all,

I *am* a grandmother now, and I don't think a granny
is supposed to make a living by getting up in front
of thousands of people, pretending to be a teenager!"
and rush back to my seat among the yetis
and Sasquatches of the high-altitude section

of the Comunale auditorium, where, as far as I can tell,
the di Lammermoors and their friends and enemies and kinsmen
and -women and *their* friends and enemies are staying well
this side of the beauty trap as they brandish weapons and roar,
"Ah love hair," "She love me," "Ahmo keel hair,"

"Ahmo keel dem all," "Ahmo fock dem all," "Ahmo keel
and fock dem all," "Dey all keel me," and so on, thus mixing your love
and sex and physical attraction with your mayhem, your menace,
your death, as though Signor Donizetti were taking into account
the utterance of his trans-Alpine not-quite-contemporary

Monsieur Rodin, who opined, "That which
is more beautiful than a beautiful thing is the ruin of a beautiful thing,"
a lesson learned at age 14 by the first great modern actress,
Eleonora Duse, whose verisimilitudinous style was
so markedly different from the stock poses and gestures

of rival Sarah Bernhardt, the last great classical actress,
when she, Duse, rehearses Juliet's lines, saying, "Who calls? I am here.

What is your will?" as she walks through
the Palio gates of Verona and makes her way to the arena where
her family's troupe will stage the play, the setting sun

turning the ancient arena's stones a fiery red as she stabs
herself with Romeo's dagger and "the crowd let out such a roar,"
Duse writes in her memoirs, " that I was terrified,"
and an actor held a torch to her face, the flame crackling
and dripping resin and smoke as she thinks, "I am Juliet;

I am death itself." Now this is a doozy of an idea,
I'm thinking, that death and beauty lie cheek by jowl like two dogs
under the same bed, so that if one is about to pop out
and race around our chamber, why, so is the other. And how fitting
that this *aperçu* comes from one who

so wowed reporters on her American tour years later
that they coined a word based on, not a blend
of "daisy" and the '20s–'30s automobile "Duesenberg,"
as some etymologists suggest, but a corruption
of the incorruptible actress's most excellent moniker!

Joan Sutherland never got caught in the beauty trap,
though she worked it, rising from the dead in the 1960 Paris Opéra
production, the gauze and mist spreading on extra smears
of spookiness like frosting on a many-layered *gâteau au chocolat.*
Think of the price you and I pay, reader, if we waste

our time judging everything according to
external appearances, like the nephew of Sir Godfrey Kellner,
who visited his uncle one day and found him in the company
of Alexander Pope, and Sir Godfrey said, "Nephew,
you have the honor of seeing the two greatest men

in the world," to which the nephew, who was
a slave trader, announced, "I don't know how great men you may be,
but I don't like your looks. I have often bought a man much better
than both of you, all muscles and bones, for ten guineas,"
thus distinguishing himself as a savage more rude

and wolvish than any of the poor creatures in whom
he trafficked and a fool, too, for never thinking that
    that which may be seen in one way is as likely to be seen
in quite another, for example, the physical appearance of novelist
        John Gardner, whom novelist Lore Segal described

        as "the most beautiful man I've ever seen . . . with silver
hair down to his shoulders, and an upturned nose and bright blue eyes,"
    whereas *New York Times Magazine* writer Stephen Singular
wrote that Gardner was "a small, pot-bellied man, and his white hair
        falls over his shoulders, so he looks something like

        a pregnant woman trying to pass for a Hell's Angel."
Mmm! As unsavory a characterization as one might ever hope
    to dodge oneself! Though surely John Gardner's enemies,
upon seeing their foe depicted in such noisome terms, took a pleasure
        as malicious as that enjoyed by our Savior's disciples

        in their attitude toward the Magdalene, intimated to be
a weathered hag in the Gospels of Matthew, Mark, Luke, and John,
    though the Gospel of Philip says that "Christ loved her more
than all the disciples and used to kiss her often on the mouth.
        The rest of the disciples were offended . . . and expressed

        disapproval. They said to him, Why do you love her more
than all of us? The Savior answered and said to them,
    Why do I not love you like her?" Poor Jesus:
He was just days away from being nailed to the cross
        and, worse, being turned into the undeserving front man

        for every anti-Semitic Inquisitorial foam-at-the-mouth
skinhead TV evangelist to drag his pockmarked behind through
    the piazza and out to some redneck crackerbarrel of a truck-route
cathedral. Unless he, Jesus, married the Magdalene,
        as the Cathars said, and sailed to Spain. And had kids.

        And grew old and died anyway, but in the fullness of time,
and in the usual way. Now that's quite a toothsome prospect,

wouldn't you say, reader? For His present-day descendants
to be walking around Toledo—I was about to say "Spain,"
though by now they'd have made it to Toledo, Ohio,

as well! What with intermarriage, they wouldn't look
like the Jesus we know from church lithographs
and the backs of those free fans they give you at funeral parlors;
still, those kids would be not only divine but also fabulous, I'm so sure.
Meanwhile, it's cut, stab, stab, hack as Lucia murders

Lord Arturo Bucklaw and goes mad, as Edgardo prepares
for his big duel with Enrico Ashton, as the dying Lucia calls
Edgardo's name, as Edgardo knifes himself in the sweetbreads.
Death, you are a basso, puffy with noise and great bluster,
ineluctable and all that, yet, in your own way, delicious.

The Hand of Fatima

> I have written elsewhere of the urine ceremony of the Baciga; the Jon Frum cargo
> cult of Efate, in Vanuatu; the harvest bingeing on three-penis wine in rural Shandong;
> the riotous bachelor houses of the Trobriand Islanders; the diet of lightly cooked
> caribou droppings among the Naskapi Indians; ritual fellation among the Asmat;
> wife inheritance, or *chokolo*, among the Sena people of the Lower Shire River in
> Malawi (and how the widow is required to engage in sexual intercourse with the
> male relative while the husband's corpse lies nearby); and the manner in which
> people in India wag their heads negatively to mean yes.
>
> —PAUL THEROUX, *Fresh Air Fiend*

Good lord—listening to our guide Leslie in the Alhambra,
      I'm shot through by 40-year-old footage
of Baton Rouge playboy Jules LeBlanc flinging his hard hat
          into the woods off Essen Lane the night he and I
               were driving home after 12 hours of road work
and three of drinking ice-cold Busch beers,

and we've come to a stoplight, and "The Locomotion"
          comes on, and Jules jumps from behind the wheel
and rushes back to this old coupe idling behind us
      and drags out a man and wife in their mid-sixties,
             makes them dance in the middle of Essen Lane,
and they do, almost gamely, as though both half afraid

and half remembering their own silly youth—
          they wanted to get along, these old-timers,
plus they had no idea what lay ahead:
      the war, the sit-ins, the drugs, the music so painful to hear
          that it would make "The Locomotion" sound like
"Begin the Beguine" or "Stardust." And the sex!

Not the tactful coupling they'd already forgotten
          but practices the very descriptions of which
would have left them in tears.
      Remember, you could still hear "Moon River"
          and "Where the Boys Are" on the radio in those days.
The average American made $4,700 a year,

and golf was still a rich man's sport;
                    bowling was America's pastime.
Bonanza and *Candid Camera* were on TV,
            which was black and white—*life* was black and white,
                        and then the blacks became Afro-Americans,
and Fu Manchu slit himself open

with a blade-like nail, and out stepped Ho Chi Minh
                into our Western noggins
as his rangier sunburned Arab cousins had earlier,
            as had the blond and blue-eyed Visigoths,
                    the ancestors of another guide that,
on another day, I encounter in Barcelona

who's tall, who's pretty, who's a little put out
                    that no one is asking her questions
about the museum here in Barcelona,
            so I say to the tour guide, "¿Are you a student?"
                    and she says, "Yes, high study the hart,"
and I say, "¿The heart? ¿La ciencia cardiovascular?"

and she says, "No, the hart, the harchitecture . . . ,"
                and I say, "¡Ah, the hart! ¡The statues, the paintings,
the series of increasingly larger cubes placed
            equidistant across a courtyard,
                    the mound of fly-blown hamburgers
intended as a protest against further protests,

the six-inch length of dowel whittled to a point
                at one end and labeled 'Opus VII (Untitled)'!"
and she says, "No, high am meaning more
        the Goyas, the Velázquezeseses. . . ."
                And that's okay, it's good: it's "No problem!"
as the waiters say, just one more misunderstanding,

yet another contretemps to ponder even after
                the charming and knowledgeable Pepita—
new city, new guide, same half-understood language—

has taken me around the Plaza de Toros in Valencia,
                    and even ushered me into the seldom-visited chapel
where the toreros pray before the statue

of the Virgin of the Forsaken,
                    the city's patron, and taken me up
to the second floor of the bull ring and around back
            so I can look down on *los toros bravos* themselves,
                    three of whom are indifferent to my presence,
though one stands up and gives me a look

that all but says, "If I could climb, son,
                    you woulda wrote your last poem about shit
you don't understand in the first place,"
            and I try to slip Pepita a tip, and she says,
                    "¡No tip!" and I say, "¿Don't you want
to buy a ticket so you can see Julio Iglesias Tuesday night?"

and she says "¡No!" and I say
                    "¿No what: no tip or no Julio?"
and she shrugs and says, "Oh, I'm going to see Julio,
            all right—I don't like him, but. . . ."
                    Pepita is a guide guided by social custom,
as are many if not most of us, many if not most of whom

are also guided by religion, as in the case of
                    our devout Muslim brothers and sisters
who are beckoned to Paradise by the hand of Fatima
            and the five pillars of Islam its fingers betoken,
                    i.e., to believe in Allah, to pray to Him
five times a day, to give to the poor, to observe Ramadan,

and to undertake the *hajj* or pilgrimage to Mecca.
                    Thus will one pass through six heavens
in the afterlife and end up in the best, number seven,
            which numeral becomes quite the coy little digit
                    in Islamic architecture, viz.,
the Courtyard of the Lions in the Alhambra contains

124 columns. Total? Seven! Even better, says Leslie,
                    the ceiling of the Sultan's Room
in that same palace is made of 8,017 separate pieces
            of wood. Total? Seven! Oh, if only it were that easy,
                    were that . . . numerical. So much in our lives
just takes us by storm, just washes over us like a tsunami

of bits, bytes, pixels, gifs both animated and ordinary,
                    jpegs and mpegs in HTML and JavaScript,
or, *my* favorite, black marks on a white page,
            and here I refer to words like *sempiternal*
                    and *preternatural* that you've looked up
a million times, yet you still don't know what they mean.

Here I refer to the story that Hemingway tells
            of how upset his son was when the matador died
because the matador was small, as are all matadors,
            and so was the boy small, as are all boys.
                    And the boy kept saying,
"I don't like it that he was dead," and his papa,

i.e., Papa, said, "Don't think about it,"
                    and the boy said, "I don't try to think about it,
but I wish you hadn't told me because every time
            I shut my eyes I see it,"
                    and at that time Hemingway's wife
was reading aloud *The Dain Curse* by Dashiell Hammett,

and every time somebody got killed off,
                    she'd substitute the expression "umpty-umped,"
and the little boy got caught up in the silliness of the words,
            and one day he said to his papa,
                    "You know the one who was umpty-umped
because he was so small? I don't think about him now."

Poor Hemingway: he umpty-umped himself
                    one July morning in Ketchum, Idaho.
Words hadn't failed him, though, at least

till the Mayo Clinic doctors gave him
        the shock treatments, 11 to 15 in all,
that stole his memory, made writing impossible.

For the rest of us, it's the liquor of words,
        the pharmacopoeia that is in the lexicon,
that *is* the lexicon, is the infinite number
        of numbers that add up to the number seven,
            is seven, is a Goth, is a Visigoth,
is a Goya, is a guide, is all guides, is God.

—for Ignacio Messana

The Winter Dance Party

A dog with a lampshade around his neck
                is checking me out as I eat a *pastelito*
on a street corner in Valencia one windy evening,
                    and I'm guessing he's got a bobo
          and he's wearing the lampshade to keep him
from biting it, which means he's thinking of little else but,
               and now he glances imploringly at the other dogs,
as though trying to make deals with them:

"Bite my bobo for me! Bite my bobo,
               and I'll do anything you want!
Kill a cat! Tear up somebody's garden!
                   Doodoo in church—whatever!"
       But the other dogs, the tasty-fuck dogs,
the ones with papers, won't give him the time of day;
             they don't even want to be seen looking at a dog
with a lampshade around his neck,

so now he's looking at me, and he's leaning forward
              a little, and suddenly his eyes flare with the spurt
of a struck match, and it's as though he's saying,
                 "Human man! Human!
     Here's your chance to be a dog! Bite my bobo!
Then you can eat anything you want—
             you don't have to wait for somebody
to wash it or cook it or even wipe it off!

I ate a man's thumb once;
             he cut it off with a table saw when I was walking
past his shop door, so I swallowed it and ran away
              laughing while his wife screamed and chased me!
     And the smells—people think we dogs
don't like fresh bread and flowers, but we do!
            The other day a woman dropped a scarf getting on the tram—
best thing I ever smelled in my life!

So why do we roll in shit and fish heads?
                            Because we can! Ha, ha! We're dogs, dammit!
Now imagine you're old and fat:
                                        your eyes are white with cataracts,
            your skin's all patchy and scaly, you wander
into the room where everyone's gone to get away from you,
                            you crash around and bump into the furniture
and then lie down with a wheeze and go to sleep.

Then the gas begins to pour out of you:
                            it rolls across the floor in waves and rises
to everyone's eyes and noses where it stings like pepper
                            while you kick and bark in your sleep and dream
            you're a young dog again, chasing a rabbit and catching it,
and the people wave a hand in front of their face
                            and smile at each other and say, 'I love that old dog.'
I'm telling you, they'll do anything for us!

Pal of mine down the street, they cut his nuts off, right?
                            Guy says to the vet, 'I feel bad about this,'
and the vet says, 'Not to worry,
                            they've got these plastic jobs I can stick in there,
            mutt'll never know the difference.'
So now my pal's running around, they're banging
                            against his legs, he don't even know they're not his!
Prosthetic dog balls! Ah, ha ha ha! Bite my bobo!"

and just then everything begins to sag and blur,
                            and I know if I fall over, I'll drop my second *pastelito*,
the one I was saving for later, so I pull myself upright
                            even though I'm still sort of scratching and woofing
            next day when I find myself in the Museo de Bellas Artes,
where I notice that there are three different types
                            of Vigilantes de Seguridad on duty, namely,
Those With Nothing, Those With Nightsticks,

and Those With Pistols, thus representing
                            three very distinct categories of response

to Noisy, Violent, and Destructive Patrons,
                    namely, Shushing, Whacking, and Killing,
        and I'm checking out one of the guards,
and she can tell I'm onto something besides
            the Goyas, so she strikes up a conversation
in the course of which she reveals

that her husband is a guard of a higher category yet,
            for he carries an automatic weapon,
and here she brings one fist up to her waist
                    and holds the other out in front of it
        and goes, "UH-UH-UH-UH-UH-UH!"
as she sweeps the gallery of imaginary vandals
            intent on spraying political slogans or "¡Ti amo, Juanita!"
on one of the several paintings in her charge,

thus bringing understandable alarm
                    to the countenances of museum-goers within earshot,
several of whom cringe with terror
                    or raise their purses to protect themselves
        from bullets that, if they have not ripped cloth
and flesh already, nonetheless seem likely to,
            so elevated is the level of enthusiasm the señora brings
to her imaginary gunplay, so verisimilitudinous her ruse.

How beautiful is the shadow these Spanish call *duende,*
            how like it is to the food we crave
when we are weepy and spent,
                    want to chew our bodies up whole
        and swallow them, to fill a museum
with the cries of the dying.
            No wonder Robert Johnson sold his soul
to the devil, as did Paganini.

Or that Buddy Holly played his best set
            the last night of the Winter Dance Party tour,
and then the little plane crashed in the Iowa cornfield.
            No wonder that, as the joke has it,

the redneck's last words were, "Y'all watch this!"
Or that the final thing the general said to his troops
                    Was, "On your feet, you cowards, their artillery
can't possibly reach us at this dist—."

Sometimes I wish I had a machine gun.
                    But I want language, too, history, jokes.
Recorded music. Hot meals. I like libraries,
                                theaters, bookstores, though sometimes at night
            when I'm walking through this city, the wind
will blow the leaves past my feet, and I'll hear
                    a howl a few streets over and I'll think *That's a dog*
and then *That's my dog* and then *That's me.*

Se mai continga che 'l poema sacro
    al quale ha posto man e cielo e terra,
    sì che m'ha fatto per molti anni macro,
vinca la crudeltà che fuor mi serra
    del bello ovile ov' io dormi' agnello,
    nimico ai lupi che li danno guerra;
con altra voce omai, con altro vello
    ritornerò poeta.

If it comes to pass that this whale of a poem
    on which heaven and earth have worked so hard
    that it's made me skinny over the years
should overcome the cruelty that keeps me
    from the pretty sheepfold where I slept like a lamb,
    an enemy to the wolves who lay siege to it,
then with a new voice and a new fleece
    I'll come back as a poet.

                   —*Il Paradiso,* Canto XXV, 1–8

For Men Only

Emily, the deaf-and-blind shih tzu of our dear friend Victoria,
         is walking the hardwood floors
of this W. 12th Street apartment at four a.m., her nails tapping out
                  a message TO: DEAF AND BLIND DOGS
OF THE WORLD (dit-dit-dot-dot-dit-dit-dit-dit)

FROM: EMILY (dit-dot-dot-dit-dot-dit-dot-dot-dit-dit-dot)
         ACTION: PEE ON THE FLOOR—NOW!
A famous painter's nephew lives across the way, and his sons
         have these beer parties
when the folks are away and throw up off the roof,

so on a given summer evening, you *might* go to sleep to the sound
         of the famous painter's grandnephews
throwing up off the roof and you will *definitely* wake
         to Emily's senescent jazz-tap routines,
like those of a doggy Judy Garland in *Babes on Broadway*

doing an endless series of spastic ball changes and waiting
         for her Mickey Rooney to appear
in the form of a schnauzer or an Airedale, an unlikely event, since—
         well, I was going to say that no dog
will love her now, but then there's that whole syndrome

scientists call Davian behavior, the relentless sex drive noticed,
         for example, in the *Bufo marinus* frog,
those three-pounders you see hopping down Miami sidewalks
         like little suitcases and the males
of which species have been observed having intercourse

in the middles of busy highways with females
         who are not only dead
but have been flattened by the tires of vehicles tearing past
         while old Warty has his grim, lusty way
with what was once surely the fair Esmeralda,

an enchanting voluptuary then but now a crusty fly-magnet
         on the asphalt, a transformation

overlooked by the amphibian gallant whose behavior was described,
              first, jocularly in scientific literature
as Davian and, then, permanently so, so *à propos* is this term

for boundless lust which takes its name from the limerick
           about the hermit named Dave /
who kept a dead whore in his cave / and had to admit / I'm a bit
             of a shit / but think of the money, etc.
It gets better—or worse, depending on whether you're looking at it

from the linguistic or the moral viewpoint—for Davian behavior
           among birds is called Avian Davian behavior. . . .
Hmmm. To paraphrase what Maréchal Bosquet said about the charge
           of the Light Brigade, *C'est magnifique,*
mais ce n'est pas l'amour. Oh, love, love, what the hell is it anyway?

Victoria loves John, her new husband, but she doesn't love Emily,
           this old crazy dog
who wanders the apartment at night like Lady Macbeth,
            not incarnadining the multitudinous seas
with Duncan's blood but jaundicing Victoria's carpets and our socks.

Love's got a Paolo-and-Francesca part, a can't-keep-my-hands-off-
           my-baby, an if-loving-you-is-wrong-
I-don't-want-to-be-right side, but also a rational aspect,
            an emotion-recollected-in-tranquility component,
both of which I recall from the rhythm and blues of my youth

with its spraddle-legged shouters, yeah, but the calm guys, too,
           their voices smooth as cane syrup
as they sing, All you fellows, gather 'round me,
            I'm going to give you some good advice!
Sleepless, I am in Chinatown early next morning, gazing at the signs

and realizing I can't tell if I'm about to enter
           a Christian Science reading room
or a brothel, so I press my face against store-front windows
            and finally see people buying pills
and powders across a counter and go in, and the guy scowls at me

and I say I'm tired, I want something for energy,
       and he reaches behind himself
and picks up this box and bangs it down on the counter and says,
       You take For Men Only,
and I say, What's in it? and he says, You take For Men Only now!

So I start down the street with my bottle of For Men Only
       and open it and shake out a capsule
in my hand, and it's long and orange and has green spots
       like spinach and it smells the way
the yard does after you mow it, so I take one, and turn into,

I don't know, Garth Brooks. . . . I'm running all over the place,
       not feeling amorous so much
as wanting to, say, re-roof the house. I mean, I'm an older guy
       who's got it under control,
but pass this stuff out to the male population in general,

and every New York street corner would look like Bat Day
       at Yankee Stadium. Farewell to chastity!
If such a thing exists. And farewell to peace of mind, for sure.
       The chastest bachelor I know
is my son Will's hermit crab, who lives by himself in a terrarium

and eats nothing but candy, those marshmallow Easter chicks, specifically—
       oh, he'll take a little spinach dip,
if there's nothing else, but he'd rather have the candy,
       which he eats with a single spindly feeler.
He's as dainty as a maid, this crab, and might even be a maid,

but whatever he is, he brooks no nonsense from the succession
       of crab roommates Will has presented him with,
at least one of whom must be of the opposite gender, but with all
       of whom he has made war, not love.
He'd rather have that candy, and who's to say he's wrong,

for if you can't have everything the way you want, at least
       you should be able to have a snack.

Quite frankly, I don't think he's really trying, but then that's his business,
                    not mine. The people I know
who are lucky at love are pretty good at slinging it themselves,

and this includes both virtuous people and sleazeball lounge-lizard types,
                    cut-rate Romeos who come on
with the Barry White tapes and that junk about loving somebody
                    and then setting them free—
I mean, why would you want to be free of someone who loves you to pieces?

I hate to keep paraphrasing the French, but why not, almost everything
                    sounds better in French,
because it's another language, and though we'll never be able to reproduce
                    the precise sense of the original,
that's okay, because we're talking about poetry here, not science,

and far from being harmed by lacunae and uncertainties,
                    poetry is actually helped by them,
so here goes: "*La beauté sera convulsive ou ne sera pas,*"
                    said André Breton, and let love too
be convulsive or let it not be at all. Chaps, let us rise above the hermit crabs

and hermits and old blind dogs, for when we invent our truest selves,
                    the lovers we deserve will appear.
Therefore let us learn another language. Let us set our hair on fire
                    and charge into battle against a numberless foe.
Let us sail upriver. Let us eat shit, drink blood, choke on pleasure.

I hear America singing; it sounds like Little Richard.
            He says, When she winks an eye,
the bread slice turn to toast, and I dream of Jayne Mansfield.
            He says, When she smiles, the beefsteak
become well done, and I dream of Mamie Van Doren, Cyd Charisse.

Across the way, the famous painter's grandnephews
            vomit off the roof as Emily dances
through the night, hearing nothing, seeing nothing, though she too
            dreams of her lover:
Cerberus, guardian of hell, a dog's dog, three-headed and immortal.

The House of Blue Light

Little Richard comes on the TV at Gold's Gym
        and the first thing that happens is, I burst into tears,
and the second thing is, I think to myself,
            I can't sing this music, but if I could,
I wouldn't accept a smidgen of public acclaim,

not one iota; rather, I'd be like
        nineteenth-century French historian Fustel de Coulanges
entering a lecture hall to the applause of students
            and saying, "Do not applaud. It is not I who speak,
but history which speaks through me,"

and as I distract myself from my sorrow with this thought,
        pert *Today Show* host Katie Couric
tries to cut Little Richard off,
            tries to get the camera on herself so she can go on
with the program, so she waves the crew back

and walks toward them to fill the lens and get away
        from Little Richard's king-sized hullaballoo:
he's saying, "Turn me up! Turn me up!"
            and then, "All the beautiful women say, 'Woo woo!'"
and the women do say, "Woo woo!" and they are beautiful,

that crone there, this four-hundred pounder,
        then he says, "All the ol' ugly men say, 'Unnh!'"
and the men do say, "Unnh!" and they are ugly,
            they're beasts, the stockbrokers in their power ties,
even the slim, almost girlish delivery boys

are fat and hairy and proud to be that way,
        proud to be selfish and to take big craps,
and I'm crying and not sure whether I'm one
            of the beautiful ones or the ugly,
and when I tell Barbara about this later,

she says, "It's an emotional time for you,
        what with Ian going away to college,"

and I see what she means,
                        because at least part of my Gold's Gym sorrow
is due to the fact that tomorrow I'll say good-bye

to this boy I've had a steak-and-egg breakfast with
                        practically every Saturday morning of his life,
and now he's going away, which he should,
                        though why Little Richard would trigger my tears,
I have no idea, except, come to think of it,

for the strong, indeed, necessary tie between
                        pop music and sentiment, as evidenced by the last time
I boohooed like a li'l wiener while listening to pop songs,
                        which was after Roy Orbison had died
and, as part of a tribute show, the d.j. had played,

not only Roy Orbison singing "Danny Boy,"
                        or a Scottish father's farewell to his only son
when he goes off to fight in the foreign wars,
                        but also the seldom-heard reply, which is the song
Danny Boy sings at his father's graveside when he comes back

and finds that, irony of ironies,
                        while he has survived saber blow and cannon fire,
Old Age, the surest of Death's warriors,
                        has crept up on his dad and cut him down
as lethally as any of the English king's artillerymen,

and now I see Ian in his tam and his kilt,
                        leaning on his musket and salting the stones
of my grave with his bitter tears. . . .
                        My son, me, Little Richard, Roy Orbison:
it's a mishmash, for sure—

certainly it's a step into the House of Blue Light,
                        the place where Miss Molly rocks
and which is not a house of prostitution,
                        which would involve a light
of a different color altogether, but a fun house,

a good-time house, yet a house where
        the unexpected occurs, sort of like that place
Muhammad Ali called "the near room"
            whose door would open in the middle of a round,
and part of Ali would be whaling the tar

out of an opponent and part would be looking
        into that room, where he'd see orange alligators
playing saxophones and dancing snakes
          with green hats on their heads,
and he'd want to go in there, want to party

with these be-bop reptiles and groove-ball amphibians,
        when suddenly whup whup whup whup! his opponent
would remind him what he was there for,
           and Ali would have to whupwhupwhupwhupwhupwhup!
and take care of business real fast

and shower and have a news conference
        and then go home and wonder what he saw
in that room there with all that crazy stuff in it,
         including some things he's seen before
and some he's never seen and some he hopes to see again

and some he can't bear to think about
        even though he's home now, got his feet up
on the Danish Modern coffee table and a nice cold glass
         of fruit juice in his hand.
He's been *some*where, that's for sure!

He's been on an "expedition,"
        a word I heard recently pronounced
as "eks-pay-DEE-shone" by an Italian biologist
         who was telling me about his latest trip to Antarctica
and who is probably the last person to have said

this word to my face since my brother Albert
        forty-five years ago when I was seven and he ten

and we used to play this game called African Ranger
                in the woods that surrounded our parents' house,
the one we had to sell when my parents got too old

to keep it up, the two sons talking on the porch
                as the mother sweeps and tidies and the father,
who has not cried at anything since the death
                of his own parents decades earlier, sobs in the study
as he says good-bye to his books, and it is late afternoon

in the early days of winter, and there is no part of the world
                gloomier than the bayou country at that time of the year,
and Albert says to me, "Want to play African Ranger?"
                and it takes me a minute to remember the game,
which consisted of starting out on an "expedition"

but soon turned into two shirtless boys shooting blunt arrows
                into each other's hides, and I say, "Nope,"
and he says, "Me either," and the last piece of light
                falls out of the sky, and it's dark out there,
the woods are black; you could walk into them if you wanted,

and a little path would take you farther and farther
                from your old life, and soon you'd see this cottage,
and there'd be music coming out of it, and you'd look in,
                and Little Richard would be there and Ali
and Roy Orbison and yourself when you were a child

but also a teenager and a young man, too,
                and everybody'd be talking and laughing,
and somebody would look up and see you as you are now,
                and they'd all wave and say,
Hey there, we've been waiting for you, come on in.

Listening to John Crowe Ransom Read His Poetry

I am waiting for my wife to get dressed
so we can drive over to campus for
the regular Tuesday poetry reading which,
when you consider that it takes place, say,
forty times a year, means that, combined
with the readings sponsored by other groups,
there are maybe a hundred poetry readings annually
of all kinds—benefits, slam poetry contests,

even anti-poetry readings—in our little town
of less than a hundred thousand people.
So while everyone decries the dwindling audience
for poetry, I don't see it: when I was in college,
we almost never had readings, and I didn't go
to any until I was a senior and John Crowe Ransom
came to the LSU campus to read his poetry.

Ransom was pretty much it as far as
Southern poetry went—at worst, he was tied
with Robert Penn Warren—what with him being
a Fugitive poet and then a member of
the Agrarian group and, later, founder
of the *Kenyon Review* as well as author of
Chills and Fever, Two Gentlemen in Bonds,
The World's Body, and all these other great collections.

So everybody was pretty excited about his coming,
with the exception of my then-girlfriend,
who was majoring in something called
Clothing and Textiles and whom I was dating
because I thought it would be refreshing to go out
with somebody who had ideas and interests
different from mine—big mistake—and who was

now beginning to pull away from me
and all the "impractical" things I adored.
She said no, she didn't see what

the big deal was, but yeah, sure, she would
                    go along to see the famous poet since
        it meant so much to me. So I put on
my best clothes and she put on hers
                    and off we go to the auditorium,

                    where everyone is waiting, all dressed up
        as though they are at the prom.
                    In those days, men still wore coats and ties
and women wore dresses to football games,
                    so you can imagine how gussied up they are
        for a poetry reading. We find good seats
                    in the middle, and everybody else files in

                    pretty quickly, until there are maybe
        seven hundred fifty or eight hundred people there.
                    And then Mr. Ransom comes out, dapper little
white-haired guy close to eighty years old,
                    and starts reading these terrific poems:
        "Blue Girls," "Piazza Piece," "Captain Carpenter,"
and, to be sure, "Bells for John Whiteside's Daughter."
                    In his semi-ironic, semi-whimsical way,

                    Mr. Ransom is just knocking everybody out,
        even though he seems to weary as the evening goes on
                    and spends more and more time shuffling his pages
between poems. My girlfriend and I are sitting
                    behind one of my teachers, Dr. Fabian Gudas,
        who is quite bald and has a big, sweet, goofy grin,
                    and his wife, whose name is Almena Meeks.

                    And behind us is this big moron
        who is in a couple of classes of mine
                    and who impresses me as little more
than a blowhard as well as something of
                    a mystery, since he is openly contemptuous
        of literature and especially poetry,
which he clearly thinks of as a craft
                    practiced exclusively by leftists and sissies.

It is during one of Mr. Ransom's silences
that the moron says loudly to his date,
          "See that bald-headed fruit? That's my English
professor," whereupon Dr. Gudas swivels around
          and scowls directly at me, who begins
to stammer things like, "I didn't say you were
          a bald-headed fruit, Dr. Gudas; I mean,

I don't think you're a fruit. . . ."
The people around me who realize what has happened
          begin to laugh, my then-girlfriend included,
while the others begin to shush us,
          because by that time John Crowe Ransom
has started up again with "Here Lies a Lady"
or "Janet Waking" or any one of a number
          of his (and I think the word comes from

a Jane Austen novel, though I can't remember
which one) superexcellent poems. The evening
          ended badly, I'm sure, with much teeth grinding
on my part and quite a few snippy exchanges
          with my then-girlfriend, who had decided
to compound my shame by not only cataloging
          but also painstakingly analyzing a number

of minor humiliations I had endured recently
in her presence but had, until that moment,
          successfully forgotten. The funny thing
is that I don't remember anything at all
          about the fight or fights that must have ensued
and the subsequent breakup, only that
I must have broken up with my then-girlfriend
          at some point because otherwise I would be

married to her and not the woman in
the other room who is trying on different
          pairs of shoes and asking, This pair?
This pair? even though I keep saying that

the latest pair is absolutely the perfect
choice, no doubt about it. What I do remember
from that evening is the trivial though,

now that I think about it,
rather amusing exchange involving me
and Dr. Gudas and that moron,
which vignette could have been scripted
by Feydeau or Goldoni or one of the other
great *farceurs,* as well as
the less flashy but more deeply satisfying
image of the somewhat donnish Mr. Ransom

and the philosophical-fanciful tone
of his wonderful poems,
which I have decided lately
to characterize by the adjective "marmoreal,"
which means marble-like, though
in a warm manner—like flesh, in other words,
but with the immortality of statues.

I Think Satan Done It

Jerry Lee Lewis is the undead, only cooler—not even the undead
        just sit there staring and suddenly churn
barrelhouse piano as though the devil himself has his forked tail

up their butt, then dash through "Big-Legged Woman" and "Breathless"
        and "Wild One," pausing only to say, "I think Satan
done it!" when an amp goes out, all the while cheerfully interpolating

their name into virtually every song: "Other arms reach out for
        ol' Jerry Lee, / other eyes smile tenderleeee!"
thus celebrating himself and singing himself as Whitman did,

that is, not as a "single, static marble statue elevated by a pedestal,"
        as Ronald Knowles notes in *Shakespeare and Carnival:*
After Bakhtin (London: Macmillan, 1998), but as one of the "sweaty

bodies of a living carnival crowd," i.e., us, the 1,500 or so who seem to be
        recruited mainly from Jacksonville shipyards and the ranches
that begin around there and go clear down through central Florida, lots

of sunburned, bowlegged guys with Popeye forearms and definitely
        the last generation to take men's hair seriously enough
for me to look out over a sea of ducktails and pompadours anchored

by what appears to be gallons of melted yak butter yet not a single drop
        of irony, and when I ask a woman where she got her Killer
T-shirt because I want one for my wife, she says, "I made it! Here!" and starts

to peel it off as I flap my hands and say no, no! for fear that Dean Don Foss
        of the FSU College of Arts and Sciences is, as Jerry Lee
works his way through "Once More with Feeling," "Workin' Man Blues,"

and "Waiting for a Train," leaning over the balcony at that very moment
        in gleeful anticipation of just such a misstep.
Now the week before the concert, two things happened, one global

and one not: first, Sir Johnny Cash died, and, sure enough,
        Jerry Lee begins his concert by saying, "Before
we start rockin' and gettin' it and throwin' stuff and goin' to jail,

I wanna sing a song for Johnny Cash," the song being "I'm Going
        to Take My Vacation in Heaven," which brings tears
to the eyes of many of the 1,500 because of its aesthetics rather than

its expressed truth, for while the young may weep at circumstance,
        as a student's father told her recently,
the old weep at beauty because they already know the world is sad.

The non-global thing was an editor at a big-city northern newspaper
        for which I write wrote me and said I hadn't written
anything for her in a while, and did I have an idea, to which I said,

Do I have an idea! and told her I already had my Jerry Lee tix,
        so just hang in there and I'll have 800 words
on your desk by the time you show up for work Monday morning.

Back comes *her* e-mail saying, Wait, I don't know, nobody around
        here thinks he's all that important, and I reply,
N-not important?!? and tick off the facts on the fingers of my left hand,

which, even though she can't see it, I'm holding in front
        of the computer screen in classic high-school
debater mode: in the forties and fifties, Sun Records founder

Sam Phillips (deceased) changed the world forever through the music
        of Elvis Presley (also deceased), Carl Perkins
(ditto), Johnny Cash (ditto as of two days ago), and Jerry Lee Lewis,

still smokin', drinkin', and rockin'. And when I say "change the world
        forever," I think of the time I was living in Paris
and walking past the Hôtel-Dieu on Christmas Eve, and the Hôtel-Dieu

is the oldest hospital in the city, dating back to the seventh century,
        if you can imagine, but, still, a working hospital—
people having babies and heart attacks don't care if it's Christmas Eve

or not. I mean, say "oldest hospital in Paris" to a pissed-off
        French woman in her seventeenth hour of labor and see
where it gets you! Anyway, as I walk past, just about frozen to death,

I hear "Great Balls of Fire" coming out of an open second-story window,
        and when I look up, I see doctors and nurses
in surgical scrubs, just dancing their hearts out. They're swing-dancing,

complete with flash moves, and dripping with sweat and laughing
        and boogieing away all their stress and tension
and unhappiness over their inability to make people live longer,

just better, and that only for a while. The music was saving them,
        I told my editor; the music healed the doctors.
How about that, reader? How about those arguments for factual

irrefutability *and* rhetorical power, including but not limited
        to rodomontade, hudibrastics, and braggadocio,
the whole made palatable, even tasty, by a certain *je-m'en-fichisme*,

a subtle yet undeniable *je ne sais quoi*. You agree? Yes? Well,
        not that big-city editor! About an hour before
I get into my car to go to Jacksonville, she writes, "David,

I'm afraid we're just a little too snooty to commission a piece
        on what's-his-name"—okay, she didn't say
"what's-his-name," though I can't resist the substitution

because it conveys editorial indifference better than the truth would.
        And I'm not even talking about musicianship!
For as he goes from "All Night Long" to "Big Blond Baby"

and "Crazy Arms," I am thinking how, in the late eighteenth century,
        Georg Christoph Lichtenberg wrote in a notebook
that in the plays of Shakespeare "you often find remarks doing

a kitchen-hand's work in some remote corner of a sentence
        which would deserve pride of place
in a disquisition by any other writer," which would be just as true

if you substituted "Jerry Lee Lewis" for "Shakespeare," "concerts"
          for "plays," "piano playing" for "remarks,"
"song" for "sentence," my name for Lichtenberg's, our time period

for the earlier one, and "this poem" for "a notebook"!
          And then Jerry Lee says, "If God made
somethin' better than a lady—umm!—he musta saved it for himself!"

And lest anyone accuse him of failing to practice what he preaches,
          let me remind you that Mr. Lewis has married six times,
even if the majority of these unions followed the arc suggested by the titles

of such songs as "Let's Talk About Us" but then "We Live
          in Two Different Worlds" and, finally,
"She Even Woke Me Up to Say Good-Bye." According to the program notes,

"he has never claimed to be a role model." He's not? Well, that's news
          to the 1,500! For he did exactly what he wanted,
and it worked, and when it didn't work, he blamed the devil.

Jerry Lee Lewis, Jerry Lee Lewis, may you have as much fun
          in hell as you did getting there,
and if not, may the devil do as you do when you knock over a can of Sprite

and begin to laugh helplessly as you wipe it up and then hold the towel
          over your face bandanna-style and say, "This is
a stick-up!" and mug for the band as a heckler shouts, "Play something!"

and you swivel on your stool and look out as though seeing the audience
          for the first time and jerk your thumb toward
the back of the auditorium and say, "Them doors swing both ways."

I Think Stan Done It

After my poem "I Think Satan Done It" appears in
       Shenandoah, the editors at *Poetry Daily* e-mail me,
who is in Italy at the time, that they want to use it
       on their Web site, only they keep referring to the poem
as "I Think Stan Done It," so I write back to say, yeah,

sure, I'm thrilled, only religion would be a whole lot
       different if, instead of Lucifer, Mephistopheles, Beelzebub,
the Prince of Darkness, or the Angel of the Bottomless Pit,
       somebody named Stan were in charge of the Hot Place,
not to mention medieval art, most philosophy from

Aquinas forward, all literature, half of fairy tales, a lot
       of *New Yorker* cartoons, and two out of three
threats from various crones, nuns, schoolyard scolds,
       and Southern Babdis' (to use Mark Twain's phonetic
spelling) grandmas about what will happen to little boys

who don't eat their lima beans or talk back
       to their grandmas! Still, you have to love it,
don't you, reader? After all, "I Think Stan Done It"
       (which, from this point forward, will refer to
the *Poetry Daily* editors' typo rather than this poem) clearly

comes from the same fertile area in our language
       whence rise the charming slips made by children
which are the only real reason for going
       to all the bother of having them, such as referring
to "magazines" as "mazageens," and such jokes

as the one about the two English spinsters in
       the Rome hotel who call down to the front desk
to complain, in their faulty Italian, that they can't
       get warm even though there are two gladiators
in the room, or the one about their young countrywoman

who tells the French *hôtelier* she has the habit
       of sleeping on top of two mattresses, only instead

of saying *matelas* (mattress), she says *matelot*
        (sailor), thus prompting the gentleman to roll his eyes
and say, *O les anglais, quelle nation de navigateurs!*

"We're never the same at night," said the very same
        Mark Twain, and indeed the Web site editors
who kept dropping the first "a" from "Satan"
        in their correspondence with me *were* writing me
at night, given the time difference between Italy

and the U.S., though I think Twain meant, not amusing
        orthographical contretemps, but more fleshy sorts
of goings-on, like a man brushing by his friend's
        wife on the way to refresh his drink at a party
and bending to give her a nice little kiss on the mouth

and being surprised when he learns that she has in mind
        not only an entirely different kiss altogether
but one accompanied by a vigorous squeeze
        of what used to be Mr. Sleeping Pink Baby
but is now rapidly metamorphosing into

the Blue-Veined Piccolo, the Heat-Seeking Moisture
        Missile, Mr. Trouser Trout, Mr. Baloney Pony,
Mr. Locker-Room Terror, old Yummy Mr. Three
        Times the Recommended Daily Adult Allowance
of Hand-Pulled Lap Taffy!—some kind of speedy,

unplanned, half-misunderstood collision, in other words,
        one involving not only an agent but also
a recipient of that agent's actions who wordlessly
        change roles in mid-scenario in a manner
that brings not only surprise but joy to at least one

and, if they're lucky, both, otherwise why would all
        the finest jokes involve misunderstandings between
seemingly oversexed spinsterly Englishwomen
        and droll if jaded male Continental hotel clerks?
Huh? Point: you don't know. You just never know.

Non si sa mai, as they say here in Italy. One of
        the Gonzaga dukes had a green and gold maze
for a ceiling, and all through it, again and again,
        you can read the legend *Forse che si, forse che no,*
over and over again: "Maybe yes, maybe no."

Some experts claim this slogan describes the fortunes
        of war, which can go either way in the course of
a pitched battle, while others maintain it's about
        the fortunes of love, which can go either way
in the course of a fierce clench or a furtive groping!

I'm betting on war. What's the difference, though:
        just about every one of these little fortified
hill towns in northern Italy has a gate with a hole
        at the top of the arch through which defenders
would pour rocks or boiling oil on the heads of hapless

attackers. Or you could pelt them with candy instead—
        the attackers only know they've got
to rush stumbling and tripping through that gate
        and without the foggiest idea of what awaits them,
whether it's rusty nails or after-dinner mints.

My parents dealt in both commodities, I think:
        Miss Josie called Dr. Tommy "Earley" whenever
he forgot a car payment or left the milk bottle
        in the kitchen sink, Earley being the simpleton
of the little farm town she grew up in. She was just

popping off, but you don't have to have a Ph.D.
        in Early Normal Pre-Cognitive Child Psychology
Hard-Wired Frontal Lobe Attribute Studies to conjure
        a vision of my brother and me holding our sides
and rolling on the living room carpet as we imagined Dr. Tom,

with his brilliantined hair parted neatly in the middle,
        his stick-insect mannerisms, and his thousand-book library

in a dozen languages as the drooling half-wit who,
            as the locals rode into town on horse carts laden
with the tomatoes and peaches they planned to sell

at the market, could usually be seen standing in front
            of the courthouse, masturbating with one hand
and picking his nose with the other.
            What kept them together, my dad and mom? Answer:
nothing. Also, everything, and plenty of both

at the same time. The great Blaise Pascal said that if people
            knew what others said of them, there wouldn't be
four friends in the world, and how much truer is that when
            it applies to sweethearts and married folk
and the things they not only say but think and half-think

about each other. Politicians talk about family values:
            what about Manson Family values? What about the fact
that we don't have the slightest idea about what we're doing
            yet manage to do it anyway with a kind of
Così Fan Tutte-ish unarticulatable grasping at as much

of the truth as we can wrap our lunch hooks
            around at any given moment, as is the case with
the carpenter who goes to heaven and sees Jesus
            and God sitting at a desk in front of the Pearly Gates,
and God says, "Why should I let you in?"

and the carpenter says, "I've worked hard all my life
            and been a good person and I'm also a carpenter,
which means I can take care of pretty much anything
            that needs fixing," and God says, "We've got lots
of carpenters up here, so I can't really let you in unless

there's something unusual about you," and the carpenter
            gets this big grin on his face and says,
"Well, I *did* raise this son who's really, really different,"
            and Jesus leaps to his feet and shouts, "Daddy!"
and the carpenter looks at him and says, "P-Pinocchio?"

Occupation: Hero

I am watching Clint Eastwood kick some serious
Nazi tuchus in *Where Eagles Dare* and thinking,
    There has never been a bad movie with a funicular
in it, and during the commercial breaks I'm also
    reading the *Tallahassee Democrat* even though I've read it

    three times already, so this time I look at the want ads
and think, "I could be a cake decorator, I'm drug free
    and have a clean driver's license, I'd do a good job
decorating cakes, I wouldn't even need drugs!"
    or "Oh, no, I could never install gutters—I mean,

    if they were at waist level, yeah, but what if I fell?"
And then it occurs to me that I am living at the wrong time,
    that, in his day, the real Doctor Faustus was an astrologer,
alchemist, magician, *and* philosopher, as were all
    the early Renaissance scientists: Copernicus,

    Tycho Brahe, Francis Bacon, Giordano Bruno, Galileo,
Kepler. Later, Newton studied alchemy, and so did
    Goethe—why not me? If I'd lived in those days,
I'd have combined all those arts, though since that
    was the norm then for your major quester types,

    there'd have been none of the *frisson* of boundary
crossing. It takes so little to make you feel like an argonaut,
    maybe even Jason himself: you're doing yard work,
and a carful of frantic strangers pulls up—they can't
    find the ball field, and their son's game begins

    in ten minutes! It's just down the road on the left,
you say, and all day long you feel like a champ,
    whereas they forgot you as soon as they pulled
into the parking lot and the umpire cried, "Play ball!"
    Or you're grilling, and the sky is black, and your wife

says, "Better stick it in the oven!" and you say no, no,
you keep turning the meat as the drops begin
        to fall, first one or two and then a deluge,
and you fly through the door with the chicken and ribs
        sliding off the platter, and your shirt's soaked and your hair

        is in your face, but you saved the meat as Ajax would,
Hector, Achilles. Now Mr. Emerson said, "The day
        is always his who works in it with serenity and great aims,"
though sometimes the path of hysteria and piddly shit
        is the one that holds more promise. True, we don't want

        to be like the guy who pulled out a pistol in the liquor store
and shouted, "Okay, mothersticker, this is a . . . ,"
        any more than we care to resemble his comrade-in-arms,
the sergeant whose instructions to the firing squad—
        "Ready! Fire! Aim!"—are a way of life to many.

        "Live to the point of tears," said the great Camus—easy
for you to say, Albert! The best the rest of us can hope for
        might be something called Heroism By Association,
as in the case of a guy I see in a bar one night,
        and he's got this belt covered with beads and turquoise,

        so I ask him if there's a story behind his belt, and he says
it's Willie Nelson's belt, that Willie's bus driver
        went to see the proctologist and was so grateful
that he gave the doctor Willie Nelson's belt, but the doctor
        didn't care, so he gave it to his nurse, but it was a man's belt,

        so she gave it to her boyfriend, who is this guy,
whose name is Gene. Or Heroism By Default: another night,
        another bar, a vet's assistant from the Jacksonville Zoo
tells me a story that might be called "The Gorilla Wakes Up,"
        because one day they're working on this lion,

        and the lion wakes up, and the vets all run out and leave her
in the cage, and the lion chases her but is woozy

from the anesthetic and keeps falling over, and finally
she makes it out the door. A week later, they're working
        on a gorilla, and the gorilla wakes up, and all the doctors

run except one, who starts giving the gorilla more drugs
that finally put it under again, and when the woman thanks him,
        he says he couldn't help it, the gorilla had been standing
on his foot. "Every man's condition is a solution
        in hieroglyphic to those inquiries he would put,"

says the same wise Mr. Emerson as was previously cited
in the present poem, and therefore "he acts it as life
        before he apprehends it as truth." So even though we suspect
that being the top-selling car salesman on the lot for April
        is not the same as boarding a British frigate and sending

its captain and crew over the rails, still, when I go to
those carefully preserved medieval towns
        in the south of France like Moissac and Carcassonne,
I really appreciate the men who saved what I'm looking at
        now from the idiots of their generation, because when

you look at a mental picture of the whole scenario,
what you get is, on the one hand, a lot of four-color lords and ladies
        running through a landscape stuffed with serfs and Saracens
and Merlins and Morgan le Fay types and, on the other,
        yourself and a bunch of people very much like. You forget

your Prosper Mérimées and your Viollet-le-Ducs
in their soup-stained suit jackets and dusty beards,
        men who look in photos as though their main occupation
was to fuck around with their pipes yet without whom
        the south of France today would be one big *supermarché*

or used Peugeot showroom. Even their own wives
probably said, "Oh, *mon dieu*, with a name like Prosper
        or Viollet, how could he possibly be a hero,"
though the less heroic then, the more heroic later,
        possibly, for "mythology is what never was but always is,"

according to Stephen of Byzantium, and even though
he said that in the sixth century, and in Byzantium,
what do we know of the Byzantines other than what
they tell us when they come to us in our dreams
and call us demigod, Amazon, seraph, lion, prince.

Everything You Do Is Wrong

She says, "Everything you do is wrong,"
and I think, She doesn't mean that,
it's just hormones talking, or the heat,
or the fact that we're spending more
than we're making, but then I think,
She's right, everything I do is wrong,
because this is the way I myself see it,

just as, when he sculpted a self-portrait,
Michelangelo used to cast himself
in an unflattering way, in *The Genius of Victory,*
for example, in which the hero,
who is this muscular but softish figure who looks more
like an associate professor
of management information systems

who has just stepped out of the shower
after the faculty–grad student softball game
than a god or a general, is kneeling on the back
of a cur who is clearly Michelangelo,
he of the unmistakably broken nose,
and that night I dream I am looking
at a fresco of hell like the one in the Baptistery,

and one of the devils is holding a skewer
that has each of my sins on it,
not gloth and sluttony and the other five
but *my* sins, my tendency to avoid people
at parties if they're not more important
than I am, for example, or the pleasure I take
in the bad luck of my friends,

and each sin is wrinkled and purplish-gray,
like a diseased organ, and in the middle is me,
small and white, sleeping like an evil baby,

and I think, God doesn't like people like me,
but then I remember what Niels Bohr said,
which is that the opposite of a profound truth
may well be, not an error, but another truth,

and I think, I'm not so bad, I mean, dogs like me,
and I won that teaching award some years back,
and for all I know I accomplish great things
every day without even knowing it,
like Masaccio's St. Peter in the Brancacci Chapel,
legging it through town and curing beggars
just with the touch of his shadow,

and he doesn't care, doesn't even notice the beggars,
he's probably thinking about his lunch,
big sandwich, maybe, but at the moment
he's just doing his job, and the lame are dancing
with joy because they can walk now,
and the blind are rubbing their eyes with disbelief
because at last they can see,

and the scrofulous gasp as they look
at each other's faces and hands because their skin
is so beautiful, why, it's as soft and pretty
as a child's, and that's when I realize
that the woman has made a serious error,
that what she really means is,
"Everything you do is right."

My Brother the Jew

My brother Albert is driving along one Saturday
and he passes this Orthodox friend of his
    and says, "Want a ride?" and the guy says,
"Can't, it's the Sabbath," and Albert says,
        "It's okay, I'm driving," and the friend says,
"Someone might see us and think you're a bad Jew."
    What a good Jew my brother's friend is!
He doesn't even want anyone to think a bad thought.

    Now Ron, who is neither my brother nor a Jew,
good or bad, is telling me about his job
    in the mental hospital in Chattanooga
and how one day the EMTs brought in
        a Hasid who had quarreled with his brother
and then tried to kill himself by jumping into
    the Cumberland River, so they dry the guy off
and get him a gown and tranquilize him,

    and that night Ron is out drinking with his friends,
and he says what'd y'all do today, and they tell him
    they were fishing under this bridge and suddenly
they heard shouting in a foreign language,
        and the next thing you know, this bearded guy
in a black suit and hat is splashing into the water.
    Can you imagine? Somebody says, "Ain't been
no fish at all since the plant opened up downriver,"

    and then somebody else says, "Got any more
of those beers?" and then from above you hear
    somebody shout, "Mein verdammte brother is a gonif!"
and this guy flies by who looks as though
        he leapt out of Poland 300 years ago
and is only landing in Chattanooga today.
    I wouldn't have thought the Hasidim killed themselves.
And certainly not in front of the goyim.

My brother might have been that Jew, for surely
we have quarreled, as what brothers have not?
        Though I can't imagine my brother killing himself.
I think my brother would be a good Jew, even though
                he does not adhere to strict Orthodox practices.
For he does not keep holy the Sabbath,
        either the Jewish one or that of
the Roman Catholicism in which he was raised.

        For he eats pork. For he eats catfish, which,
dipped in cornmeal and lightly fried in peanut oil,
        he likes even more than pork.
For he does not keep a kosher kitchen
                but instead consumes meat and dairy products
at the same meal, as when he scarfs a cheeseburger.
        For he takes steambaths, not to indulge in the ritual
of the mikveh but to relax and get clean.

        I wonder if my brother believes in anything.
More than a few men are atheists in their youth,
        drunkards and whoremasters,
yet on their deathbeds they are all the same,
                staining the sheets with their dread
and shouting hysterically for a confessor.
        Many have tried to convert the Jews;
John Donne wrote of it,

        and Steve Swartz tells me when he broke up
with that unspeakable wife of his,
        a woman so terrible their union lasted
only six weeks, this very lovely fiftyish
                black woman who was the branch manager
at his bank said, "Honey, let me tell you something—
        you need to get Jesus into your life
and that bitch the fuck out."

        Why, I myself was married to a Jewish woman once,
and since rabbinical law says the religion
        of the mother determines that of the children,

I am therefore, though not Jewish myself,
                    the father of Jews, like Moses or Abraham.
Yet my two sons know nothing of Judaism—
            are bad Jews, though not as bad as the dad and uncle
who have so neglected their spiritual upbringing.

            What is a good or bad Jew? Or good or bad person,
for that matter? And who's to say.
            In graduate school, I had a violinist for a neighbor,
and when he practiced, the other students,
                    the wise guys in Educational Leadership
and Information Systems Design, would slap
            the walls or grab brooms and thump the ceiling
and shout, "Cut that out, we're studying here!"

            The year before, he'd lived in a low-rent building,
where his neighbors were mostly retired Jews,
            blue-collar types, tailors and shopkeepers,
and he'd rub resin on his bow and start to saw away,
                    and when he paused, he'd hear the doors opening
in the hall. So he'd practice for an hour or two,
            and when he put his instrument down,
he'd hear the doors close again, softly, one by one.

Teacher of the Year

This year last year's Teacher of the Year
        broke an office window having sex with a student
at Laurie's university, Laurie tells me,
        and I say, "Ummm . . . broke it with what?"
and she says that's what everybody wants to know,
        like, the head? The booty? The consensus is

it was a foot bobbing UP and down and UP
        and down and then lashing out in a final ecstatic
spasm, crash! Then comes surprise, giggles,
        and shushing noises. Somebody finds out,
though. Somebody always finds out:
        my first Mardi Gras, when I was ten,

I remember passing a man saying,
        "Oh, come on, baby, why can't we let BY-gones
be BY-gones?" and shaking his cupped hands
        as though he is comparison-shopping
for coconuts while peering pleadingly
        into the pinched face of his female companion,

whose own arms are folded tightly across her chest,
        and even then I thought, Hmmm! Bet I know
what those bygones are! I.e., that they have
        nothing to do with who ate that last piece of cake
or brought the car home with the gas tank empty
        and everything to do with sex stuff.

Laurie is in town with Jack, who is a therapy dog,
        and she tells me she takes Jack to homes
and nursing centers to cheer up old-timers,
        and after their first visit, she asked
the activities coordinator if she should do
        anything differently, and the woman says,

"Could you dress him up?" And Laurie says,
        "Excuse me?" and the woman says,

"They really like it when the dogs wear clothes."
        My analysis: having seen people act like dogs
all their lives, toward the end, elderly folks
        find it amusing when dogs act like people.

A German shepherd could be Zorro, for example,
        and a chow Elvis as a matador. A poodle could be
St. Teresa of Avila, a border collie Sinatra.
        A yorkie could be a morris dancer
and a sheltie a gandy dancer or vice versa.
        A schnauzer could be Jayne Mansfield.

Dogs could pair up: imagine a boxer
        as Inspector Javert chasing a bassett hound
as Jean Valjean under the beds, around
        the potted plants, in and out of the cafeteria.
Or a bichon frisé as Alexander Hamilton fighting
        a duel with a Boston terrier as Aaron Burr.

On the romantic side, there could be
        a golden lab and a chocolate lab
as Romeo and Juliet or a Samoyed and a husky
        as Tristan and Isolde, though it wouldn't be good
to let their love end the way doggie love does:
        the posture isn't nice, and the facial expressions

are not the kind of thing you want to think about
        when you're thinking about this kind of thing.
Up to a point, you want to know it all,
        then the more you know, the less you want to know.
Though you can't help wondering:
        a shoulder? An elbow? A knee?

Dead Girl Takes Packet Boat to Provincetown

All day long we keep running into that dead girl:
coming out of Congdon's Pharmacy
      with her sunblock and lip gloss, tearing down Main
with her backpack-wearing boyfriend in tow, racing into
         Espresso City for a double decaf skim-milk frappucino.

      She's pretty lively for a dead girl, which is how
we think of her ever since we'd seen her the night before
      in Nantucket's Actors' Theatre production of Marsha Norman's
'Night, Mother as Jessie, who lays out these meticulous plans
         for the suicide her mother begs her not to commit

      with the earsplitting BANG! you hear just before
the curtain, a finale so convincing you're sure
      there'll be no actress out there smiling and bowing
just a few seconds later, yet there she is,
         brains intact, pleased at all the applause, obviously,

      and probably thinking already of the trip to Provincetown
she'll be taking today if she can just get her errands done,
      just field one or two more compliments from people like us,
saying, "Hey, glad to see you're alive and all!" and reply,
         "Thanks, but I gotta catch that boat to Provincetown!"

      I see former U.S. Surgeon General C. Everett Koop
earlier in the day, he of the unmistakable helmet-strap beard
      and resolute visage of an Ahab, though his foe
was lung cancer and heart disease, not the White Whale.
      When I realize it is him, I want to say,

      "Way to go, Mr. Surgeon General, sir! Way to fight
the good fight against teenage smoking, even if it's made a comeback
      since your post was filled with less-determined public officials!"
But I don't say anything, and when I tell locals who I've seen,
      they say, "A lot of guys around here look like him."

Some are alive, some aren't, and some are in between,
like Miss Josie, my 97-year-old mother,
          who says her favorite thing is sleeping: some days
she stays in bed the whole time, though her daytime snoozing
          is not the same as the nocturnal variety;

          it's better, she says, because when it's dark out,
she just sleeps ("I was unconscious for 12 hours last night," she observes,
          "and nobody knew it, not even me"),
whereas during the day, she wakes often to reflect on
          the nap she's just had and the one she will take directly,

          and even as she tells me this, she is dozing off,
her chin dropping by degrees to her chest,
          a little smile still playing about her lips.
Certainly, none of us is immortal—well, the two old men
          of Nantucket are, the first being

          he of the prodigious anatomy and the second
he who kept all his cash in a bucket and whose daughter named Nan
          ran away with a man, and as for the bucket, etc.
Death hath no dominion, but even if it does,
          you can't take your bucket with you.

          The reason we are in Nantucket in the first place
is to see the world première of my play *Mrs. Kaneshiro Sees God,*
          a singular experience for a first-time playwright
who is watching others give life to words
          he has written, not to mention the unsettling business

          of running into my characters on the street,
such as my Bobby, the surfer who dies offstage
          and who, in real life, is Nantucket carpenter Tommy Folby,
a much handsomer Bobby than I'd ever imagined,
          more . . . all-American. Speaking of which,

          when he hums "The Star-Spangled Banner" in the play,
half the people in the audience start to stand up—

what can they be thinking? Though at the cast party after,
I myself keep calling the actors by their characters' names
("My name's Martina, David, not 'Deb'!").

To get to the island, you can catch a boat,
like the suicide girl, or you can take a little ten-seater,
flown, in our case, by a dumpy, unhappy-looking guy
who introduces himself as "Curtis"—I'm thinking,
what's wrong with "Captain Flanagan"?

Curtis asks us how much each of us weighs
and then bends over and puts his hands on his knees
and has a coughing fit. I figure Curtis for two,
maybe three packs a day; it's the only time I ever want
to ask a pilot what his cholesterol level is.

Speaking of a sensible diet, right after
I run into former U.S. Surgeon General C. Everett Koop,
I order a lobster roll at the lunch counter
in Congdon's Pharmacy, and the woman next in line says
she wants one, too, but only if it doesn't contain celery,

and I say, "You're allergic to *celery*?" and she gives me
a look, so I say, "Well, I'm allergic to cats!" and she says,
"Yeah, I die if I eat it—I'm allergic to an enzyme in celery,"
and I think of the time Barbara took me to the emergency room
and say, "I guess I'm allergic to an enzyme in cats. . . ."

What is death, anyway? According to Melville,
it's "a speechlessly quick chaotic bundling of a man into eternity,"
like, you're standing by the taffrail, puffing on your pipe,
and a big wave comes by, or your leg gets tangled in a rope,
and buh-bloopedy-doop! You're up there with God

and the two old men of Nantucket, the one with the grin
and the other with the bucket of cash he managed
to smuggle in somehow, and all the teen smokers are there,
still smoking, and the suicide girl, who must have missed her boat somehow,
and Bobby the surfer, a.k.a. carpenter Tommy Folby,

and the lobster-roll woman—turns out
the Congdons' "secret family recipe" has celery
in it after all, only nobody told the counter guy.
Yes, and Curtis is there, and he's tanned and fit;
he's flying 747s now, and he's going back for another load

of—what shall we call them? Not "the dead," surely;
they look so alive. Halfway between God's big whale-ship
and the earth, he'll pass Miss Josie, smiling and sleeping
as she floats through skies of cream and cerulean,
little white feet together, little hands crossed on her breast.

Calling Robert Bly

We're reading "In Danger from the Outer World"
in my graduate seminar and somebody asks,
            "I know what all the bad stuff in the poem is—
the fire, the water, the plane crash, the grave—
            but what's this 'shining thing' inside us
that 'shakes its bamboo bars'?" and I say,

            "Umm, the unconscious mind?" and somebody else says,
"Maybe it's the soul," and a fourth person sneers
            and says, "A poet like Robert Bly wouldn't believe
in a stupid idea like that," and the third person
            says, "You're not Robert Bly, how do you know
what Robert Bly believes?" and the fourth says,

            "You're not me, how do you know what I know?"
so to keep the peace, I interrupt with
            the standard English professor's joke:
"Hey, too bad we can't just call the poet up
            and ask him what he meant, huh?"
and then I think, Wait a minute,

            we're not talking about Wordsworth here,
and since it's break time anyway,
            I say, "Okay, everybody, come on up
to my office, we're gonna call Robert Bly!"
            and I leg it upstairs with my students
shuffling along behind and grab my copy

            of the *Directory of American Poets* and sure enough,
there's a Robert Bly in a town called Moose Lake,
            Minnesota, and I dial the number,
and a woman answers, and I say, "Can I speak
            to Robert Bly?" and she says, "Just a minute!"
and then this voice at the other end says, "Hello!"

            and I say, "Mr. Bly?" and the voice says, "Speaking!"
and I introduce myself and we chat a bit and then

I tell him we're reading this poem of his
called "In Danger from the Outer World,"
        only nobody gets this one image, and can he
explain it to us, and he says, "Aw, you know!

    It's the soul or the human spirit—something like that!"
I turn to the students, but by this time most of them
        have drifted away to the bathroom or the coffee machine,
so I cover the receiver and say to no one,
        "Mr. Bly says I'm right—it is the unconscious mind!"
and I look out the window as far as I can

    and imagine Robert Bly sitting there with his phone in his hand
and all of America between us, the line
        going out through Benevolence, Georgia, where a woman
who has just finished baking a buttermilk pie
        for a family dinner the next day
decides it isn't enough and starts to make a second;

    then on to Difficult, Tennessee, where one man
has just sold his car to another and is now taking
        a photo of the new owner alongside his new vehicle;
then Knob Lick, Kentucky, where a man is having sex
        with a woman who is younger than he is
and doesn't love him anymore, though she hasn't told him yet;

    and Goreville, Illinois,
where two men tell a third they're going to whip his ass,
        and he startles them when he shrugs and says,
"Go ahead"; and then Vesper, Wisconsin,
        where a child is dying of acute myeloid leukemia,
and his parents can't do a thing about it.

    In the darkness outside Robert Bly's cabin, a moose
is cropping ferns, his leathery flap of an upper lip
        closing over the fronds as delicately
as a lady's hand picking up a tea cake,
        and he looks up, startled, when Robert Bly
laughs at something I've said, and then

Robert Bly says, "How are your students—are they any good?"
and I say, "They are, though they seem
                a little tired tonight," and he says,
"Are they good writers?" and I say,
                "Yeah, most of them," and he says,
"How about you—you a writer?"

        and whatever I say makes Mr. Bly laugh again really loudly,
but this time the moose just keeps on eating,
                finishing its little patch of ostrich ferns
and sniffing the night air and thinking, Umm—asparagus!
                and then stepping off, graceful as a skater,
toward the lake it can't see but knows is there.

Borges at the Northside Rotary

If in the following pages there is some successful verse or other,
may the reader forgive me the audacity of having written it before him.
    —JORGE LUIS BORGES, foreword to his first book of poems

After they go to the podium and turn in their Happy Bucks
        and recite the Pledge of Allegiance
and the Four Truths ("Is it the Truth?
                Is it fair to all concerned? Will it build good will
and better friendships? Will it be beneficial
        to all concerned?"), I get up to read my poetry,

and when I'm finished, one Rotarian expresses
        understandable confusion at exactly what it is
I'm doing and wants to know what poetry is, exactly,
                so I tell him that when most non-poets think
of the word *poetry*, they think of lyric poetry,
        not narrative poetry, whereas what I'm doing

is narrative poetry of the kind performed
        by, not that I am in any way comparing myself
to them, Homer, Dante, and Milton,
                and he's liking this, he's smiling and nodding,
and when I finish my little speech,
        he shouts, "Thank you, Doctor! Thank you

for educating us!" And for the purposes
        of this poem, he will be known hereafter
as the Nice Rotarian. But now while I was reading,
                there was this other Rotarian who kept talking
all the time, just jacked his jaw right through
        the poet's presentations of some of the finest

vers libre available to today's listening audience,
        and he shall be known hereafter as the Loud Rotarian.
Nice Rotarian, Loud Rotarian: it's kind of like Good Cop,

Bad Cop or God the Father, Mary the Mother.
Buy Low, Sell High. Win Some, Lose Some.
    Comme Ci, Comme Ça. Half Empty, Half Full.

But in a sense the Loud Rotarian was the honest one;
    he didn't like my poetry and said so—not in so many words,
but in the words he used to his tablemates
    as he spoke of his golf game or theirs
or the weather or the market or, most likely,
    some good deed that he was the spearchucker on,

the poobah, the mucky-muck, the head honcho,
    for one thing I learned very quickly
was that Rotarians are absolutely nuts
    over good deeds and send doctors to Africa
and take handicapped kids on fishing trips
    and just generally either do all sorts of hands-on

projects themselves or else raise a ton of money
    so they can get somebody else to do it for them,
whereas virtually every poet I know, myself included,
    spends his time either trying to get a line right
or else feeling sorry for himself and maybe writing a check
    once a year to the United Way if the United Way's lucky.

The Nice Rotarian was probably just agreeing with me,
    just swapping the geese and fish of his words
with the bright mirrors and pretty beads of mine,
    for how queer it is to be understood by someone
on the subject of anything, given that,
    as Norman O. Brown says, the meaning of things

is not in the things themselves but between them,
    as it surely was that time those kids scared us so bad
in Paris: Barbara and I had got on the wrong train, see,
    and when it stopped, it wasn't at the station
two blocks from our apartment but one
    that was twenty miles outside of the city,

and we looked for someone to tell us how
            to get back, but the trains had pretty much stopped
for the evening, and then out of the dark
            swaggered four Tunisian teenagers,
and as three of them circled us, the fourth
            stepped up and asked the universal ice-breaker,

i.e., Q.: Do you have a cigarette?
            A.: *Non, je ne fume pas.*
Q.: You're not French, are you?
            A.: *Non, je suis américain.* Q.: From New York?
A.: *Non, Florida.* Q.: Miami?
            A.: *Non, une petite ville qui s'appelle Tallahassee*

dans le nord de . . . And here the Tunisian kid
            mimes a quarterback passing and says, *Ah,*
l'université avec la bonne équipe de futbol!
            He was a fan of FSU sports, of all things,
so we talked football for a while, and then
            he told us where to go for the last train.

Change one little thing in my life or theirs
            and they or I could have been either the Loud Rotarian
or the Nice one, and so I say to Rotarians everywhere,
            please forgive me,
my brothers, for what I have done to you
            and to myself as well,

for circumstances so influence us
            that it is more an accident
than anything else that you are listening to me
            and not the other way around,
and therefore I beg your forgiveness, my friends,
            if I wrote this poem before you did.

NOTES

"Preface": The critical essay referred to here is Peter Klappert's "The Invention of the Kirby Poem," *Southern Review,* 36 (Winter 2000).

"Stairway to Heaven": The anthology with Judith Kitchen's introduction is *Isle of Flowers: Poems by Florida's Individual Artist Fellows* (Tallahassee: Anhinga Press, 1995).

"Fair Creatures of an Hour": The title is taken from "When I Have Fears That I May Cease To Be," by John Keats. The names of actual people have been altered here as they have been elsewhere in these poems.

"Dear Derrida": For a fuller treatment of this paradigm-changing moment in cultural history, see my essay "What Is a Critic?" in *What Is a Book?* (Athens: University of Georgia Press, 2002).

"My Dead Dad": Just so no copy editor will be blamed unjustly, it should be confirmed here that the title of this poem is not "My Dear Dad," which is how it has occasionally been reprinted by those who cannot imagine that any poet would title his work so callously.

"Americans in Italy": It's the nature of these poems to tell not only the story but also everything behind the story. In this case, though, I'd be remiss if I didn't give credit to the man who provided the image in the last two stanzas of this poem. His name is Gary Winegardner, though he performs professionally under the name "Bashful."

"I Think Stan Done It": After the editors of the *Denver Quarterly* accepted an essay of mine on mistaken identity called "I Never Said What They Say I Said, or Everything You Always Wanted to Know About Pull Quotes But Were Afraid to Ask," they asked if I had a poem on the subject they could run as a companion piece, and this is it. Readers interested in the essay will find it in my book *Ultra-Talk: Johnny Cash, the Mafia, Shakespeare, Drum Music, St. Theresa of Avila, and 17 Other Colossal Topics of Conversation* (Athens: University of Georgia Press, 2007).

"Teacher of the Year": R.I.P. Laurie O'Brien (1949–2004), the bravest and the best-natured.

Printed in the United States
109648LV00002B/24/A